Christ and Consumerism

GW00503784

Christ and Consumerism
Critical reflections on the spirit of our age

Edited by
Craig Bartholomew
and
Thorsten Moritz

paternoster
press

First published in 2000 by Paternoster Press

06 05 04 03 02 01 00   7 6 5 4 3 2 1

Paternoster Press is an imprint of Paternoster Publishing,
P.O. Box 300, Carlisle, Cumbria, CA3 0QS, UK
Website: www.paternoster-publishing.com

British Library Cataloguing in Publication Data
A catalogue record for this book is available from the British Library

ISBN 0-85364-987-1

Cover Design by Gert Swart and Zak Benjamin, South Africa
Typeset by WestKey Limited, Falmouth, Cornwall
Printed in Great Britain by Biddles Ltd, Guildford, Surrey

Contents

Contributors

Craig Bartholomew is an Anglican minister and a research fellow at Cheltenham and Gloucester College of Higher Education. He specialises in Old Testament wisdom literature and philosophical hermeneutics. He is the International Director of the Christian Worldview Network and heads the Scripture and Hermeneutics Seminar.

Graham Cray is Principal of Ridley Hall, Cambridge, a Church of England theological college. Previously he was vicar of St. Michael-le-Belfrey in York. His special concerns are the church's mission to postmodern culture and strengthening the theological foundations of the charismatic movement. He is married to Jackie and they have two daughters.

Colin D. J. Greene is Head of Theology and Public Policy at the British and Foreign Bible Society. He is the author of *Christology and Atonement in Historical Perspective*, published by the Open Theological College, and has taught systematic theology and doctrine at Trinity Anglican Theological College, Bristol. He previously served as an Anglican minister in urban contexts in the diocese of Leicestershire. He is married with three children.

Gordon McConville comes from Northern Ireland. He studied Modern Languages at Cambridge and Theology at Edinburgh, before doing a PhD on Deuteronomy in Belfast and settling into Old Testament teaching in Bristol, Oxford and now Cheltenham. He and Helen have four children, grown up (but still around). They (not the children) enjoy mild forms of exercise and suffer bouts of Francophilia.

Thorsten Moritz moved from Germany to England in 1987 to pursue doctoral work at London University. He is Senior Lecturer in New Testament at Cheltenham and Gloucester College of Higher Education and has written on Ephesians and Luke's Gospel. A further main interest of his is to rethink ecclesiology biblically. He, his wife and their son Dominic Ute are part of a house church.

Nigel Scotland is Field Chair in the School of Theology and Religious Studies at Cheltenham and Gloucester College of Higher Education where he has lectured since 1984. He was chaplain and lecturer at the College of St Paul and St Mary, Cheltenham, from 1975 to 1984. Before that he served as rector of the parish of Lakefield in the diocese of Montreal. He is the author of *Charismatics and the Next Millennium* and *Sectarian Religion in Contemporary Britain*.

Alan Storkey teaches at Oak Hill College and has studied the economics and sociology of consumption and consumerism. His doctorate at the Free University, Amsterdam, dealt with the epistemological foundations of consumption theory and he has done other work on family economics. His sociological study has involved the personal and family dynamics of consumer culture. His wife, Elaine, leaves most of the shopping to him.

Gordon Wenham is Professor of Old Testament at Cheltenham and Gloucester College of Higher Education and has written commentaries on Genesis, Leviticus and Numbers and co-authored *Jesus and Divorce*. Married with four children, he is also a lay reader in the Church of England and enjoys gardening.

Foreword

Scott M. Peck's wonderful book, *The Road Less Travelled*, begins with the memorable sentence 'Life is Difficult'. I want to respond by adding that mission is difficult. It is so, because Jesus calls us to be both in our own culture – understanding its passions and attractions – as well as to be deeply counter-cultural in our relationship with that same culture. The horizon of heaven calls us to be deeply dissatisfied with our own times as well as to embrace and redeem them.

The attractions of an age of plenty, with its obvious benefits, at least for many if not for all, presents some unique difficulties for the contemporary missionary. The temptation has often been to present the Christian faith as something which is 'relevant' to the present age. After all, who would wish to be accused of being irrelevant? But the temptation to explore relevance can lead all too easily to a presentation of the faith as merely a more attractive product to be desired, experienced and consumed. As the pages of this thoughtful work make clear, the church has all too easily been seduced by the consumerism of our age. Christians have sought to compete rather than to challenge. The 'Faith-Word' movement amongst Charismatics most clearly illustrates this tendency with its 'name it and claim it' or, as some have described it, 'blab it and grab it' theology.

The more costly alternative is to strive for a deeper credibility for the faith. Credibility drives us towards a union of spirituality and mission. All too often in church history the quest for spirituality as a goal in its own right or activism in mission as pure pragmatism have pushed mission and spirituality to function without one another. Whenever there is such a separation there lies a danger in the extremes of unhealthy isolation from the culture or undue seduction by it.

As I read the pages that follow, I had in mind a particular question. Is this volume only a critique of consumerism or does it move beyond an examination of the problem? Do the authors provide an inspirational resource that allows the reader to find wells of hope from which the missionary imagination can draw?

There are a number of important elements which suggest to me that the contributors have positively addressed such a concern. First, they draw deeply on the biblical text as a powerful narrative that directs us to the God who calls the people of God to pilgrimage, rather than to the barricades. Second, they have a clear grasp of the contours of Christian tradition which can never escape the call to authentic community as a context of individual fulfilment. That tradition is deeply informed by an awareness of a Trinitarian commitment as representing a true vision of God.

Third, they insist that there is an ethical dimension to the Christian faith which flows from the nature of God and which can never accept a merely pragmatic accommodation with the prevailing culture. This is not to say that the authors have fallen into the facile trap of offering answers, still less, 'seven step' programmes that we might adopt. Such a response would merely reflect a consumerist response to consumerism itself.

This attempt to draw on the resources of Bible and tradition to inspire an engagement with the culture of the coming century represents a particular decision. It runs counter to the advice of those who suggest that we need to re-interpret the Bible and tradition so that it more closely conforms to contemporary demands. I suspect that in the last few years we have just crossed the delicate boundary that recognises that the radical voices which have counselled the abandonment of tradition are actually the guardians of a lost past, rather than the prophets of an emerging future. It has ever been thus. If church history teaches us anything at all, it reminds us that the pioneers who have helped the church to transition from one age to another have always relied on orthodox faith as the radical interpreter of the coming context. The contributors to this volume stand in such a tradition.

Dr Martin Robinson,
Director of Mission and Theology,
British and Foreign Bible Society

Preface

Relentless consumerism characterizes the First World today. If Jesus is right that we cannot serve both God and mammon (Luke 16:13), it follows that Jesus' followers today simply *must* examine their priorities in life lest we unwittingly take on the spirit of our age. These essays aim to contribute to that process of critical examination. This is not a 'How to survive consumerism as a christian' manual – it was never intended to be. Nor is it comprehensive in trying to analyse every aspect of consumerism. We are a group of Christian academics who have tried to address some of the main aspects of consumerism from out of our particular specialities.

In the introduction Craig Bartholomew sets out the challenge that consumerism presents to Christians today. Colin Greene examines the different ways in which Christ has been understood to relate to culture and seeks out a model that will be fruitful in our time. Gordon McConville looks at how the Old Testament presents challenges to consumerism and Thorsten Moritz does the same with the New Testament. Craig Bartholomew seeks to establish a way of reading the Bible that inoculates Christians against consumerism. The development of contemporary economics and the question of how we have arrived at our present situation is considered by Alan Storkey. Gordon Wenham interrogates the ethics of consumerism and Nigel Scotland explores the relationship between the church and consumerism. Finally Graham Cray critically explores the connection between consumerism and the Toronto blessing.

We are grateful to Pieter Kwant for helping us to conceptualise this volume in the first place. In the process of developing this book in February 1998 we held a conference at Cheltenham and Gloucester College of Higher Education entitled 'Seduction or

Evangelism?' It revolved around the relationship between the gospel and consumerism. Over 150 local Christians responded to the invitation to meet for a day of listening and discussing. We are grateful to the School of Theology and Religious Studies for hosting that conference and for its contribution to this volume (two of the papers from that day are included in the volume).

We have enjoyed working together on this volume and express our thanks to Paternoster, all the contributors, and to Isobel Stephenson for her help with final editing. Our desire is that *Christ and Consumerism* will contribute in some way to helping us follow Christ more faithfully at the start of a new millennium.

Craig Bartholomew and Thorsten Moritz

1

Christ and Consumerism: An Introduction
Craig Bartholomew

If 'culture' refers to the way we shape and develop our societies, and includes such things as banks, schools, leisure, political parties, homes, movies, malls and restaurants, then it is obvious how deeply embedded we all are in culture. Although to a significant extent humans shape their culture, we also live in it, and it is mostly as natural to us as the water in which a fish swims. Often, it is only when we travel to a different culture that we become aware of ourselves as cultural beings.

It is this naturalness of culture that makes it difficult to develop a critical perspective on our culture. Growing up in South Africa, as I did, a society structured along racial lines and privileging 'whites' seemed normal. One grew and developed and exercised one's humanity in this culture, and it required a real effort for a white South African to begin to see just how abnormal the culture was.

However, for God's people to live effectively as his people, it is crucial that they reflect critically on the culture in which they live. God calls us to be salt and light in our societies, to restrain evil and to promote good, but we will only be able to do this if we are aware of the forces and ideologies shaping our culture and are starting to see where the real battlegrounds are in western culture today. This is not to suggest that western culture is inherently evil, but it is to deny that it is inherently good. Like all of life, western culture is fallen and as capable of misdirection as any other culture. Christians who pray 'Your will be done on earth as it is in heaven' ought to have a keen interest in contemporary developments in our culture so that we can discern what to support and what to oppose in our efforts to do God's will.

Failure to engage in such cultural analysis will not leave us unaffected by our culture. One of the myths of much twentieth-century evangelicalism is that one can be *acultural*. One *can* ignore one's cultural context, but it is impossible to escape it. Indeed, if we ignore our culture we will be destined simply to reproduce it and, as Dean Inge warned, those who are wedded to the spirit of this age are destined to be widowed in the next.[1] Taking God seriously and being zealous for the reputation of his character in our day will mean asking what time it is in our culture; it will mean testing the spirits of the pervasive cultural winds that blow so strongly around us.

This book is a collection of essays exploring *a*, if not *the*, spirit of our age, namely consumerism. Susan White describes this spirit as follows:

> Sociologists tell us that people interpret their lives through basic narratives, that provide a framework within which to understand the world and to establish goals and values. If there is any overarching metanarrative that purports to explain reality in the late 20th century, it is surely the narrative of the free-market economy. In the beginning of this narrative is the self-made, self-sufficient human being. At the end of this narrative is the big house, the big car, and the expensive clothes. In the middle is the struggle for success, the greed, the getting-and-spending in a world in which there is no such thing as a free lunch. Most of us have made this so thoroughly 'our story' that we are hardly aware of its influence.[2]

Similarly, Steven Miles says of consumerism that a 'parallel with religion is not an accidental one. Consumerism is ubiquitous and ephemeral. It is arguably *the* religion of the late twentieth century.'[3] Miles notes how pervasive consumerism is, affecting our cities, our homes, our lives.

---

[1] Wells, *Wasteland*, 221, expresses this in terms of consumerism as follows: 'Evangelism without a worldview is simply marketing with no purpose other than a desire for success and no criteria by which to judge the results other than mounting numbers of warm bodies.'

[2] White, 'Story', 4.

[3] Miles, *Consumerism*, 1.

White's and Miles' comments need unpacking in a number of ways. It is worth noting why at the end of the twentieth century it is so easy to make consumerism – 'the narrative of the free-market economy' – our story. Communism appears to have collapsed, consumer capitalism has triumphed and appears to be settling down for a long stay. A consumer culture in a western-style democracy appears to be the only viable option. Francis Fukuyama has even argued that free-market democracy is the goal towards which history is headed so that in this sense we are at the 'end of history'.[4] In the renaissance of the Labour Party in the UK we have witnessed a remarkable embrace of consumerism and democracy under the guise of *new* Labour.[5] The alignment of consumerism with democracy makes it hard to see why we should be too worried about getting into bed with the spirit of *this* age. Harrisville and Sundberg's words are salutary in this respect:

> Recently, the left and all its reflection in Marxist structure has collapsed, leaving the entire inhabited world a candidate for free enterprise. But with this change the demonic has not ceased to exist – neither in the world, nor in the church. And who is to say whether or not that evil spirit will bring in to this house swept clean seven other worse than himself?[6]

And indeed, the demise of communism should not obscure from us the crisis that capitalist modernity has got us into. The reaction to modernity that post/late modernism represents alerts us, for example, to the environmental destruction that modernity has bequeathed, and to the widespread embrace of nihilism in the west.[7]

---

[4] See Fukuyama, *End*.

[5] See Miles, *Consumerism*, 10f.

[6] Harrisville and Sundberg, *Bible*, 261.

[7] For an important analysis of nihilism and postmodernism see Milbank, *Theology*, especially chapter 10. I prefer to describe postmodernism as *late* modernity because it seems to me that what we are seeing are the implications of modernity working themselves out. Thus the nihilism of postmodernism is not *post*-modern but an expression of the secularism of modernity.

We urgently need, therefore, to ask more detailed questions about consumerism as the overarching narrative structuring our lives at the end of the twentieth century. How have we reached this point? Is consumer*ism* something new – part of what is being called *postmodernity* – or is it simply the dominance of the market in the modern world and therefore part of modernity from its inception? And what precisely are the key elements of consumerism?

Consumerism is new *and* old.[8] We should certainly guard against seeing consumerism as something entirely new, popular as this view is at present. Slater argues convincingly that modernity and consumer culture are inextricably interwoven from the inception of modernity.[9] He points out that the core practices of consumer culture originated in the seventeenth and eighteenth centuries, which he calls early modernity, so that consumer culture is not a product of industrialisation but underlies modernity.

> In so far as 'the modern' constitutes itself around a sense of the world experienced by a social actor who is deemed individually free and rational, within a world no longer governed by tradition but rather by flux, and a world produced through rational organization and scientific know-how, then the figure of the consumer and the experience of consumerism is both exemplary of the new world and integral to its making.[10]

Slater finds the roots of consumer culture in the commercial revolution of early modernity. As early as the sixteenth century a wide dispersion of consumer goods in the lives of different social classes is evident; fashion and taste are becoming key elements of consumption and infrastructures that target these markets are being developed. Of course industrialization played a key role in the development of consumerism, and Slater notes that the development of mass production of consumer goods took place between 1880 and 1930. The 1920s was the first decade to proclaim a

---

[8] It may be useful to make a distinction between consumption and consumerism or between commerce and consumerism. For the former distinction and a very useful discussion of the emergence of consumerism see Miles, *Consumerism*, 3–12.

[9] Slater, *Consumer*.

[10] Ibid., 6.

generalised ideology of affluence and the 1950s and 1960s became 'the period of the economic miracle that was so directly experienced in rising consumption standards'.[11] The introduction of the credit card in 1950 may be seen as symbolically marking the transition to consumerism.[12]

It is this period that Andrew Walker describes as

> the defining moment in modernity, when it passed from its early to its late phase. . . . Beginning in the United States, and heralded in the 1940s by Henry Ford, consumerism has become the dominant cultural force of the last half of the century. . . . After the Second World War, rising standards of living, full employment, technological advance, and innovative marketing spearheaded the American revolution that has led to its cultural dominance and imitation ever since.[13]

Clearly consumerism does not arrive in the 1980s with postmodernism. However, there is an intensification of consumer culture in the 1980s. The 1980s saw the collapse of communism and the capitulation of the eastern block to consumer culture.[14] It was a time of radical individualism, exemplified by Margaret Thatcher's statement that there is no such thing as society but only individuals and their families. According to Slater:

> The 1980s also heralded the subordination of production to consumption in the form of marketing: design, retailing, advertising and the

---

[11] Ibid., 11.

[12] So Whiteley, *Design*.

[13] Walker, *Telling*, 143.

[14] Slater, *Consumer*, 36f., explains that 'what emerged so harrowingly for Western socialists in 1989 was the extent to which Eastern citizens had indeed come to see consumer freedom exercised through the market as both the epitome and linchpin of all other freedoms. . . . To the eyes of the Western left, the scenes of millions of ordinary citizens turning to the street throughout the cities of the East to refuse a corrupt system in the name of civic freedom was a truly heroic return to enlightened modernity. The speed with which this was swept aside in favour of an identification of all freedom with the right to go shopping over the Berlin Wall was terrifying . . . civil society meant consumer society, civic freedom the freedom to shop freely.'

product concept were ascendant, reflected in postmodern theory as the triumph of the sign and the aestheticization of everyday life.[15]

This intensification is intimately related to the communications revolution under way and embodied in the Internet.

Slater is right to locate the roots of consumer culture in the commercial revolution in early modernity. And certainly it is wrong to see consumerism as distinctively post-modern. From the perspective of consumer culture, postmodernism can be seen as the triumph of capitalistic modernity.[16] However, I suggest that we ought carefully to distinguish commerce from consumer*ism*. It is possible to see commercial development within culture as healthy while seeing consumerism as an unhealthy development of commerce. In order to be able to make this distinction, we need to recognise the characteristics of consumerism.

Firstly, consumerism points to a culture in which *the core values of the culture derive from consumption rather than the other way around*. A capitalist consumer economy spills over into all other areas of life where it metaphorically exercises undue control. Miles is referring to this when he suggests we distinguish consumerism from consumption by understanding consumerism as the psycho-social impact of the consuming experience.[17] As Slater says:

> If there is no principle restricting who can consume what, there is also no principled constraint on *what* can be consumed: all social relations, activities and objects can in principle be exchanged as commodities.

---

[15] Slater, *Consumer*, 10.

[16] See Alan Storkey's chapter in this volume and Wells, *Wasteland*, 218. Any comprehensive analysis of postmodernism has to take account of the continuity between modernity and postmodernity that consumerism represents. Wells rightly notes that some authors, such as Thomas Oden and Diogenes Allen, understand modernity in exclusively intellectual ways . . . and they overlook the enormously powerful social realities that have created a world in which Enlightenment humanism seems so plausible. . . . The dominance of these social processes is really the key to understanding one of the chief characteristics of the post-modern person. This person, fashioned by modernity, is a *consumer*.

[17] Miles, *Consumerism*, 5.

This is one of the most profound secularizations enacted by the modern world.[18]

Related to this radical secularisation is what scholars describe as the aestheticisation of commodities; the appearance of products becomes crucial because products provide the basis for the negotiation of meaning and personal identity. Slater perceptively notes the influence of romanticism in contemporary consumerism. Romanticism criticised early consumer culture, but

> paradoxically romanticism also bequeathed to consumer culture many of the themes that we consider most modern or postmodern. . . . The very idea that acts of consuming are seriously consequential for the authenticity of the self . . . is an unintentional consequence of these early developments, as are many of the 'authentic values' in which modern consumer goods come wrapped: naturalness, emotional gratification, ethnic and national cultural values, images of innocent children, natural women and happy domesticity. It is through romanticism that consumer culture becomes both wildly playful and deadly earnest.[19]

Thus relationships, for example, rather than being the basis for an economy, start to become a marketable product. Take sexuality, for example. From a Christian perspective, sexuality is a gift from God that finds its most profound expression in the context of a marriage relationship in which it gives expression to the oneness of the bond. Pornography has always turned sexuality into a marketable product. But nowadays advertising and the Internet intensify this process in an unprecedented way.[20] A significant percentage of the Net is made up of sites providing pornography, so that the individual

---

[18] Slater, *Consumer*, 27.

[19] Ibid., 16.

[20] Bauman, *Postmodernity*, 23f., notes how consumerism undermines the relational safety nets in society: 'The changing pragmatics of interpersonal relations . . . now permeated by the ruling spirit of consumerism and thus casting the other as the potential source of pleasurable experience, is partly to blame: whatever else the new pragmatics is good at, it cannot generate lasting bonds, and most certainly not the bonds which are *presumed* as lasting and *treated* as such.'

consumer can access whatever he or she desires from anywhere in the world day or night.

Secondly, in consumerism *freedom is equated with individual choice and private life*. Slater notes that freedom to choose is the correlate in modernity of the Enlightenment understanding of reason as a private resource that the individual was encouraged to use against the irrational social authority of tradition, religion, etc.[21] Freedom of choice is in principle unconstrained and for the sake of private pleasure. The implications of this are radical. Freedom to choose whichever carrots you like in the market is one thing. But the extension of this freedom to choose whatever 'product' you like in any area of life is altogether another. And yet the tendency of a consumerist culture is in this direction. The American literary theorist Stanley Fish notes that 'all preferences are principled and all principles are preferences. . . . In short, one person's principles are another person's illegitimate (mere) preferences.'[22]

Consumerism's mixture of freedom, individualism and Fish's sort of pragmatism, combined with the suspicion of reason so typical of postmodernism, is a potentially explosive and dangerous cocktail of ingredients. One reason why this mix is so dangerous is identified by Zygmunt Bauman, who asserts that

> the switch from the project of community as the guardian of the universal right to decent and dignified life, to the promotion of the market as the sufficient guarantee of the universal chance of self-enrichment, deepens further the suffering of the new poor – adding insult to their injury, glossing poverty with humiliation and with denial of consumer freedom, now identified with humanity.[23]

Bauman also argues that those who are not prepared to be seduced by the market are the dirt of contemporary society.[24] For the 'seduced', consumerism becomes a source of liberty, for the former, who cannot afford this liberty, it becomes repressive.[25]

---

[21] Slater, *Consumer*, 28.
[22] Fish, *Change*, 11f.
[23] Bauman, *Postmodernity*, 23.
[24] Ibid., 14.
[25] Bauman, *Freedom*.

Thirdly, a consumerist culture is one in which ironically *needs are unlimited and insatiable*. Ironically, because consumerism promises to satisfy our needs in an unprecedented way, but its continuance depends on that satisfaction never actually being achieved: 'market society is therefore perpetually haunted by the possibility that needs might be either satisfied or underfinanced.'[26]

These characteristics are widely recognised by students of consumerism. While it would be wrong to ignore the positive side of consumer culture – the relatively widespread affluence it provides, the real choices it makes possible – it is surely clear that from a Christian perspective, the move from consumer culture to consume*rism* is fraught with danger. In their book on the church and consumerism, Kenneson and Street rightly say:

> We believe that the church is called to be a sign, a foretaste, and a herald of God's present but still emerging kingdom. Because the hallmark of that kingdom is God's reconciling work in the world, the church lives to point to, to embody, and to proclaim that reconciling work. But because this present-but-still-coming kingdom is a certain kind of kingdom, the church is called to be a certain kind of people. Not just any kind of community will do. If the convictions that animate the life of the church are at cross-purposes with the convictions at the heart of this coming kingdom, then the church will fail to be what God has called it to be. If the church's embodied life and witness are to be a sign, a foretaste, and a herald of this kingdom, then the church must strive diligently to embody faithfully those convictions that make visible this kingdom.[27]

A kingdom perspective and not a consumer perspective must shape the life of God's people. But this is easier said than done; we become so used to our consumer culture that it seems natural and right, and we allow it to reshape all aspects of our lives. And the church is not exempt from this danger. A growing chorus of voices warns that Christians are letting consumerism shape their core values rather than letting a Christian perspective shape their consumption. In *God in the Wasteland* David Wells argues that American evangelicals

---

[26] Slater, *Consumer*, 29.
[27] Kenneson and Street, *Church*, 23.

are allowing consumerism to reshape their faith so that God becomes the author of our satisfaction and the God of mercy becomes a god at our mercy.[28] From a different perspective, Sardar castigates Don Cupitt's religion of love as follows: 'Cupitt's postmodern religion amounts to little more than a feeble attempt to legitimate white man's lust. It also replaces Christian domination with market imperialism. His alleged pluralism hides the merciless authoritarianism of the market; which amounts to a celebration of the West.'[29] The British sociologist Zygmunt Bauman argues that fundamentalism is a specifically postmodern form of religion, forged as a 'radical remedy against that bane of postmodern/ market-led/consumer society – risk-contaminated freedom'.[30]

However we evaluate them, these different perspectives alert us to the fact that in an increasingly consumerist society it is vital that Christians maintain their integrity and reflect on the positives and negatives in different parts of our culture as consumerism pervades these areas. David Wells is surely right that 'when the church abandons the biblical worldview, when it fails to confront its culture with this worldview in a cogent fashion, it has lost its nerve, its soul, and its *raison d'être*.'[31] Such an engagement must be comprehensive. As an ideology consumerism seeps unremittingly into every area of our lives and it will need to be screened in every area. Take tourism, for example. It is great to have umpteen packages to choose from in the high street travel shops, but what are the global implications of this kind of western consumerism? Ziauddin Sardar argues in his fascinating *Postmodernism and the Other* that 'tourism is consumerism writ large, naked and unashamed, and to feed the insatiable need of tourists whole nations are converting themselves into vast emporia, havens of everything under the sun that can be bought.'[32] The implications of this type of consumerism are often very destructive for local communities.[33] Strikingly Sardar contrasts pilgrimage with

---

[28] Wells, *Wasteland*, 114.
[29] Sardar, *Postmodernism*, 249.
[30] Bauman, *Postmodernity*, 184.
[31] Wells, *Wasteland*, 223.
[32] Sardar, *Postmodernism*, 138.
[33] Ibid., 136, refers to the example of Thailand's Pee Pee Island.

tourism, noting that pilgrims bring back blessings whereas tourists take back souvenirs.

To pray as Jesus taught his disciples, 'Your kingdom come, your will be done on earth as it is in heaven' must come down to thinking critically about things like tourism and education and leisure from a Christian perspective. These are, after all, deeply influential elements of that earth for which we pray. Critical Christian reflection on consumerism is no easy task. The essays in this volume are a contribution to the ongoing challenge to Christians to discern the spirits at work in western culture at this time.

Bibliography

Bauman, Z., *Freedom* (Milton Keynes: Open University Press, 1988)

—, *Postmodernity and its Discontents* (Cambridge: Polity, 1997)

Bocock, R., *Consumption* (London: Routledge, 1993)

Fish, S., *Doing What Comes Naturally: Change, Rhetoric and the Practice of Theory in Literary and Legal Studies* (Durham: Duke University Press, 1989)

Fukuyama, F., *The End of History and the Last Man* (London: H. Hamilton, 1992)

Harrisville, R. A. and Sundberg, W. *The Bible in Modern Culture: Theology and Historical-Critical Method from Spinoza to Käsemann* (Grand Rapids: Eerdmans, 1995)

Kenneson, P. D. and J. L. Street, *Selling Out the Church: The Dangers of Church Marketing* (Nashville: Abingdon, 1997)

Lyon, D., *Postmodernity* (Buckingham: Open University Press, 1994)

Milbank, J., *Theology and Social Theory: Beyond Secular Reason* (Oxford: Blackwell, 1990)

Miles, S., *Consumerism as a Way of Life* (London: Sage, 1998)

Sardar, Z., *Postmodernism and the Other: The New Imperialism of Western Culture* (London: Pluto, 1998)

Slater, D., *Consumer Culture and Modernity* (Cambridge: Polity, 1997)

Walker, A., *Telling the Story: Gospel, Mission and Culture* (London: SPCK, 1996)

Wells, D., *God in the Wasteland: The Reality of Truth in a World of Fading Dreams* (Grand Rapids: Eerdmans; Leicester: IVP, 1994)

White, S., 'A New Story to Live By?' *TransMission* Spring 1998, 3–4

Whiteley, N., *Design for Society* (London: Reaktion, 1993)

2

Consumerism and the Spirit of the Age
Colin Greene

The consumer society of late modernity revels in stories of economic and financial success. Time magazine publishes the latest list of self-made billionaires. The personal fortune of Bill Gates, the entrepreneurial owner of the software giant Microsoft, has now exceeded fifty billion dollars. National lotteries reward devotees with instant millionaire status, offering a new twist to the rags-to-riches dream of consumer capitalism. More and more of us invest our savings in company shares and bonds and then anxiously scrutinise the erratic behaviour of the stock exchange. Similarly, as Jeff Gates recognises in his recent and seminal book:

> We are all now buffeted by a global economy in which key actors are encouraged, even mandated, to maximise financial returns in a world-wide auction of sorts in which financial values have become a substitute for the values of ethics, religion and community.[1]

An interesting spin on the apparent success of consumerism is the fascination we have with certain spiritual gurus whose self-help remedies are commodified and sold to the stress-ridden victims of the free-market economy. An example of such a person was the late Sir Lawrence van der Post, one-time spiritual advisor to both Lady Thatcher and Prince Charles. His lifelong search for personal spiritual values that combined a respect for individuals with the preservation of the environment symbolises one of the major

---

[1] Gates, *Ownership*, xix.

dilemmas facing the exponents of consumerism at the end of the twentieth century. Many are not aware, however, that Van der Post's spiritual pilgrimage was born out of a clash of cultures that was to make an indelible impression on him throughout his life and, more to the point, offers a cameo of the dangers and opportunities presently facing the Christian church.

Van der Post was raised in Africa and one of the dominant concerns of his life was his great love and affection for the Bushmen of the Kalahari desert. His grandfather had taken an active part in the virtual extermination of the Bushmen because of their annoying habit of killing and eating the settlers' cattle. Van der Post was horrified by this example of genocide within his own family tree. In the 1930s he began to hear occasional reports from hunters of small groups of desert nomads who could survive for long periods without regular food and water in the most inhospitable terrain. Van der Post set out in search of these Bushmen and he it was who both discovered their whereabouts and reintroduced them to the world at large through his books and natural history programmes. But, ironically, the success of these programmes has resulted in a new threat to the Bushmen's way of life, for tourists come to see them and the government of Botswana now intends to turn the land where they are living into a national game reserve.

The precarious existence of the Kalahari Bushmen is a particularly poignant and all-too-familiar story in the context of the modern world. It illustrates the conflict that so easily arises between the desperate attempt to preserve the rights and way of life of a pre-modern society and that of other natural species threatened by the ravages of modernity, and the pressure to pander to the interests of the exotic tourism that is a particular feature of the image-driven culture of postmodernity.

Like the Bushmen, the Christian faith originated in the context of pre-modernity, where it demonstrated a remarkable ability to survive despite recurring attempts to eradicate it. It then reluctantly entered into a perilous accommodation with the advocates of modernity that both introduced it to the obsessions of the market place and greatly endangered its future, hemmed in as it now is on every side by the capitalist consumer game reserve of postmodern culture. We must turn our attention to a more detailed examination of this predicament.

Three Models for Cultural Engagement

One of the greatest difficulties the church faces as it seeks renewal and a new future is a loss of confidence in its own identity. This is because our existing ways of being church are collapsing and we are losing the structures that previously undergirded the church's engagement with its cultural context. My starting point, therefore, is to look at three models that have historically been used by the church to locate its self-identity and define its relationship with the prevailing culture.

The Apostolic Model (Acts 1:8)

The first major paradigm is that provided by the book of Acts. 'But you will receive power when the Holy Spirit comes on you; and you will be my witnesses in Jerusalem and in all Judea and Samaria, and to the ends of the earth' (Acts 1:8). The rest of Acts describes the fulfilment of that commission. The pouring out of the Spirit at Pentecost produced the communitarian fellowships of Jerusalem. The first wave of persecution to hit the church propelled the nascent Christian community into Judea. The first evangelistic mission undertaken by Philip established the church in Samaria, and the conversion of the apostle Paul and his subsequent missionary journeys took the gospel to the rest of the world. The book of Acts clearly implies that the missionary expansion of the church is still an unfinished agenda, one which the 1910 Edinburgh conference on world mission thought to be achievable by the end of this century. In the light of the dramatic decline of the church in the first world at least, that sentiment has proved to be somewhat over-optimistic. Nevertheless, this is an agenda that is still ours to fulfil. The apostolic model has four primary characteristics:

Koinonia
Churches were intensely loyal and committed groups of believers, who shared their corporate life at a variety of levels (Acts 2:42–47). Most certainly they shared prayer, worship and apostolic teaching, but they also shared close personal relationships and systems of economic interdependency. They understood themselves to be the *ekklesia*, the community who lived by reliving the stories and

teachings of Jesus. They were, in the words of one modern theologian, 'a discipleship of equals'.[2] Entry into these churches was not self-selecting but, increasingly during the later apostolic period, through a rigorous process of initiation and teaching that established the new convert in the apostolic faith of the Christian community. This faith was based on the conviction that the Messiah had come in the person of Jesus and that his death and resurrection signalled the advent of the end times.

Diakonia

Responsibility and service were the hallmarks of the early churches. Responsibility for maintaining unity in the face of internal discord and strife was coupled with a willingness to seek the anointing of the Spirit who would equip the saints for works of service and the building up of the body of Christ (Eph. 4:11–13). This responsibility was also, as Bruce Winter indicates, to follow Jeremiah's injunction to the Jews in exile and seek the welfare of the city. This was the early Christian understanding of *politeia*, one which was eschologically oriented and ethically motivated:

> To stand in the true grace of God demanded a deep commitment to the welfare of the city within the framework of a living eschatological hope. That enabled the Christian to place personal concerns second to the needs of others in the city. This firm, eschatological hope of a secure inheritance meant that their present or impending suffering would be no ultimate catastrophe for them (1 Pet. 4:12).[3]

Diaspora

The ever-present reality of suffering meant that the church did not stagnate or become over-satisfied on a diet of self-congratulatory worship and introverted fellowship. Instead, churches spawned other fellowships and were propelled out into uncharted territory. This happened due to the impulse of the Spirit, and in the face of sporadic cycles of intense persecution that prevented any roots being established too deeply (Acts 8).

---

[2] Fiorenza, *Memory*, 140–154.
[3] Winter, *Welfare*, 19.

Martyria

Martyria is, of course, the Greek word from which we derive the English word 'martyrdom'. This was the defining category for the relationship these apostolic communities had with their cultural environment. The church witnessed to a crucified and risen Christ in a culture that was perceived as enemy territory. The culture was hostile and antagonistic to the new Christian faith, not least because the church refused to swear political allegiance to the Roman empire. To preach Christ as Lord was regarded as political sedition. Therefore some Christians endured the same fate as their leader and were crucified as birthday presents for the emperor whom they had defied by locating ultimate authority in the person of Jesus the Christ.

In the last thirty years of this century the first three of these characteristics of the apostolic church have been revisited and reappropriated by many individuals and churches involved in the charismatic renewal. This movement has produced burgeoning networks of new churches with their own distinctive revival of apostolic ministry, communitarian lifestyle and church planting. Similar patterns have been evident, although in a more restrained fashion, in the historic denominations. However, the last characteristic of the apostolic model is often conveniently forgotten by those who are trying to resurrect this model as the one that most fits our contemporary situation.

The culture we inhabit may not be gospel friendly, it may have abandoned its origins in the Judaeo-Christian faith long ago, but this is not a culture that imprisons and crucifies believers. The relationship between church and contemporary culture cannot be reduced to a simplistic model of believer versus antagonistic persecutor. That is why all the combative imagery of taking enemy territory, overthrowing principalities and powers, and binding territorial spirits does not ring true. The reality of spiritual warfare in terms of an ever-present vigilance in the face of systemic evil should not be trivialised by resorting to such language to define the church's relationship with its cultural context.[4] The interface between church and culture is much more sophisticated than the battle imagery allows. Contemporary culture consists of some who

---

[4] In this regard see Wink, *Powers*, 37–63.

are antagonistic, others who are genuinely interested, many who are indifferent and many more who remain to be convinced. Moreover another, later paradigm makes it impossible to disregard the lessons of history and simply try to resurrect the attitudes of which we read in the pages of the New Testament.

The Christendom Model: *AD 313–1648*

The Christendom model began in AD 313 with the conversion to Christianity of the emperor Constantine. The vestiges of this model, which replaced the apostolic one in the era between the first few centuries and the religious wars that tore Europe apart at the end of the sixteenth century, are still with us. If the apostolic model defined the church's relationship to its cultural environment in terms of subversive resistance, the Christendom model defined it as peaceful co-existence. The central, defining characteristics of the church were dramatically altered:

Koinonia

Small, committed and essentially egalitarian communities of believers were replaced by an expanding network of parish boundaries. The church now sought to define its relationship to the host culture in terms of territorial responsibility. Previously, few people were Christian; now, in theory, everyone was. Mutual interdependence was replaced by anonymity and nominalism. The discipleship of equals increasingly became a hierarchy. The teaching and initiation of converts was replaced by rites of passage for every citizen.

Diakonia

Diakonia was translated into the conviction that it was the responsibility of all to be good citizens of the empire, to conform to its laws and uphold its cherished traditions. The charismatic dimensions of ministry and service were replaced by the professional services of clerics. The active political engagement of the laity was superseded by the powerful political advocacy of bishops, patriarchs and popes.

Diaspora

Due to the absence of persecution, there was no longer any need for the flexible response mechanisms of the early church. Gone were the communities of sojourners and 'resident aliens',[5] replaced instead by organised religion. The church settled down to a long period of cosy co-existence with the representatives of Christendom, be they monarchs, popes, politicians and at times theologians, with only the monastic movement and the religious orders holding out for a more authentic form of Christian discipleship.

Martyria

The notion that all were witnesses with allegiance to one overlord was supplanted by the notion of citizenship because there was no longer any need for mission. Indeed the missionary expansion of the church was replaced by the imperialistic advancement of the empire. The greatest loss of the Christendom model was the eradication of any missionary interface with culture, so the church became indistinguishable from its cultural landscape:

> The church moved from being a small, persecuted minority to being a large and influential organization; it changed from harassed sect to oppressor of sects; every link between Christianity and Judaism was severed; an intimate relationship between throne and altar evolved; membership of the Church became a matter of course; the office of the believer was largely forgotten; the dogma was conclusively fixed and finalized; the Church had adjusted to the long postponement of Christ's return; the apocalyptic missionary movement of the primitive Church gave way to the expansion of Christendom.[6]

The Pluralist Model: *AD 1648 – Present Day*

If the apostolic model was 'the church resistant to culture', and the Christendom model was 'the church married to culture', then the pluralist model was the capitulation of the church to culture. One of the consequences of the Enlightenment was that church and state were overtaken by other forces that effectively demanded a new relationship between the two. The peaceful concord between empire and Christianity was shattered by the Reformation and the

---

[5] Hauerwas and Willimon, *Aliens*.
[6] Bosch, *Mission*, 237.

religious wars that followed in its wake. The baleful experience of Christendom effectively devouring itself had a profound effect upon its subjects. The ability of the Christian faith to offer a unified worldview and so provide political and social stability for its peoples came to an end, giving way to the emergence of the nation state. It now became the business of the state or the monarchy to decide which religious confession would hold sway for the majority of its subjects, be that Reformed, Anglican, Roman Catholic or Lutheran.

Pluralism in religious belief produced an important intellectual development. If Europe could tear itself apart in the name of religion, was this because the Christian faith was not based on divinely inspired doctrines after all, but was a human invention that obscured rather than illuminated what it meant to be human? So emerged the faith of secular humanism with its fundamental affirmation of the omnicompetence of human reason, the right of individual self-determination, the belief in historical progress, and the eventual appearance of the market economy. All of which brought about the displacement of the Christian faith from the public sphere and the marginalisation of the Christian church as the custodian of a privatised religion.

The kind of world that resulted from this movement to modernity is well described in the following summary:

> The Enlightenment is the source of the intellectual ferment that resulted in the technological marvels of the late 20th century. It has also promoted the exercise of instrumental reason, lauded human domination over the natural world, and at least made it more difficult for human beings to draw nourishment from the more communitarian of their impulses.[7]

To this should be added the rise of capitalist economic expansionism and the advent of the consumer society. The apparently insatiable demand for an endless variety of commodities and the erratic and unpredictable expansion of capital has inevitably led the church down the same consumerist route.

---

[7] Lakeland, *Postmodernity*, 13.

Consequently, we should not be surprised that in reality the pluralist option was, in part, the attempt by some forms of Protestantism to reinvent the apostolic model. The church was to be understood once again as the community of the faithful seeking refuge from a largely hostile environment. For others, notably liberal Protestants and Roman Catholics, it was simply the extension of the Christendom model into a new cultural context. The church was still for the people of the nation, be they believers or, in the words of Schleiermacher's title, the 'cultured despisers of religion'.[8] What we have in fact inherited is bits and pieces of both the apostolic and Christendom models, put through the reductionist grinder of the pluralist option. Pick-and-mix religion was not invented by advocates of the New Age, it has been around for at least two hundred years as the diversity and multifarious options of the pluralist model have formed themselves into a veritable consumer bonanza. The situation is well described by Peter Berger:

> The religious tradition, which previously could be authoritatively imposed, now has to be marketed. It must be 'sold' to a clientele that is no longer constrained to 'buy'. The pluralist situation is, above all, a market situation. In it, the religious institutions become marketing agencies and the religious traditions become consumer commodities.[9]

The church has, consequently, struggled to redefine adequately its relationship with the culture of scientific and technological humanism. Numerically the church continues to decline and its social and political witness is accordingly impaired. Wilbert Shenk graphically describes the contemporary malaise that effects us all:

> Renewal will not be realized by modulating dissonances between culture and church. And neither can it be achieved by urging the restoration of the original New Testament pattern or by appealing for the reinvigoration of tradition regardless of how noble a particular variety may have been. New structures, appreciation of culture, the original New Testament pattern of the church, and respect for

---

[8] Schleiermacher, *Religion*.
[9] Berger, *Canopy*, 138.

ecclesiastical traditions are all important. But none of these options offers an adequate basis for revitalizing the church that now subsists in the lengthened shadow of Christendom.[10]

Cultural Engagement and Cultural Dissonance

So what are the characteristics of the church that are still tied to some, if not all, of these previous models of cultural engagement? They are threefold and they all produce a great sense of cultural dissonance.

The Problem of Credibility: The Apostolic Model

The main problem with the attempt to rehabilitate the apostolic model is that the more the church perceives its fundamental relationship with contemporary culture in terms of antagonistic or subversive opposition, the more it tends to withdraw into its own cultural ghetto. The marginalisation of the Christian churches and their complete inability to engage creatively with the presuppositions and values that undergird contemporary culture has been much in evidence ever since the state took over from the church as the custodian of public life. We cannot delude ourselves that becoming a Christian is also the process whereby we divest ourselves of our cultural skin. There is always a tension, sometimes creative, sometimes destructive, between our Christian faith and the values of contemporary culture. Our response to this tension shapes our missionary engagement with contemporary culture.

Despite the impressive growth of some evangelical and charismatic churches, there are an increasing number of Christians who now see themselves as post-evangelical or post-church because they cannot sign-on any longer to the kind of religious schizophrenia that masquerades under the title of 'Bible-believing Christian'. That is because many of our churches offer neither an appropriate spirituality, nor a credible practical theology to sustain them in their daily encounters with contemporary culture.

---

[10] Shenk, 'Mission', 154.

It is what the Americans refer to as the 'baby boomers' and 'Generation X' who have by and large deserted the churches. Some find their way into experimental or alternative worship churches, but most simply opt out of what is, for them, no longer a credible form of Christian discipleship.

The Problem of Accessibility: The Christendom Model

There are other reasons why baby boomers continue to absent themselves from the churches and other forms of organised religion, and are involved instead in Buddhist meditation groups and New Age 'DIY religion'. They view the church as hierarchical, patriarchal, hopelessly traditional and, what is worse, quite simply boring. By and large, this group prefer to be egalitarian rather than hierarchical, gender-inclusive rather than patriarchal, informal and flexible rather than traditional, and personally engaged rather than bored.

The marriage between church and state upon which the Christendom model was founded transformed the church into the custodian of the values and aspirations of the empire. But the divorce brought about by the Enlightenment, leaves any church that still adopts this model looking hopelessly out of date, an inaccessible relic of a bygone age. The nonconformist churches suffer less in this regard, but even here the paraphernalia of Sunday worship, church governance, and the practice of ministry appear to bear witness to a church marooned in the traditions of a previous era.

The Problem of Plausibility: The Pluralist Model

In the midst of a culture that has worshipped at the shrine of pluralism, a church that merely apes the spirit of the age looks increasingly implausible. A pluralist society tolerates one and all as long as none of the players puts forward an exclusive claim for truth. How can the church venture into the public arena when its diagnosis of and prognosis for the state of society are viewed as nothing more than the babbling of the chattering classes? How can the church endeavour to speak with one voice if evangelicals, charismatics, liberals and fundamentalists each have their own particular brand of the truth, and all the brands appear equally unpalatable and implausible to those listening from the outside?

The sociologist Peter Berger referred to the fact that each culture creates its own plausibility structures through which it tries to make sense of the world.[11] Take, for instance, the debate about human sexuality. It is, of course, a vexed and difficult subject, but if the church adopts a sloganist position that simplifies the issues and pillories those who think otherwise, then we begin to look hopelessly implausible to those who, from the vantage point of their own sexual orientation, have agonised over the issues for a long time. If genuine ecumenism means anything, it surely means helping the church to speak what it believes to be the truth in a sensitive and compassionate manner to those who may still beg to differ.

The Postmodern Model: The Shape of Things to Come

What will the church look like in the twenty-first century? That we are in a state of profound cultural crisis, few would deny. This situation has led some people to adopt the 'church in exile' model as an appropriate way to conceive of the relationship between the church and postmodernity. For example, Raymond Fung, the former Evangelism Secretary for the World Council of Churches, suggested that the present relationship between the church and culture is rather like the parable of the prodigal son.[12] Modern culture is dissipating its energies and using up its spiritual and moral reserves in a capitalistic revel of monstrous proportions. The church, like the Father, just has to wait until an economically bankrupt, morally chastened and spiritually exhausted modern culture once again returns to the fold of mother church. To many, this looks like wishful thinking.

If we use Jesus' description of discipleship as like salt or light, then we find a model best described in terms of the critical interaction of church and culture. The agenda for this interaction is not determined by the world, however, but by the very nature of the

---

[11] Berger, *Imperative*, 136–148. For an astute critique of how Berger uncritically assumes his own plausibility structures, see Lesslie Newbigin, *Foolishness*, 10–17.

[12] Fung, *Agenda*.

message the church proclaims and the self-identity of the church as the primary witness to the crucified and risen Christ. The gospel is the reality and hope of the coming reign of God and the church is the living embodiment of that hope and promise that is ultimately aimed at the healing of the nations. Only through close attention to this mandate can the church hope to free itself from slavery to market-driven consumerism. What then would be the contours of such a critical interaction between the church and contemporary postmodern culture? Here are a few suggestions.

The Return of the Church to the Public Domain

The church must once again discover what it means to speak prophetically and profoundly in the public domain. The judgement of modernity upon the church is that it is best understood as a privatised utility dispensing a franchised commodity called 'religion'. Many contemporary cultural analysts regard that commodity as capable of being packaged and dispensed to satisfy a variety of tastes and personal preferences. It can be raves in the nave for the young and trendy, charismatic sweet-talking with Jesus for the hurt and self-indulgent, austere ritualism for the aloof and conservative, evangelical biblicism for the out-of-sorts moralisers and complainers, self-help meditation for the introverted and confused, syncretistic mysticism for the effete and intelligentsia, and radical social action for the disillusioned and disenchanted.

All of which may be of interest to those in the club, but it cuts no ice with those whose business it is to determine what goes on in the public square. The present Bishop of London has recently criticised the tendency to view God and religion as a commodity to be marketed to potential consumers.

> If you start thinking in terms of customers and churches being supermarkets, dealing in a commodity called God, then the essence of the Christian faith, which is a personal relationship with the divine, can very easily get lost in power play and marketing strategies, so it is a terrible blasphemy to make a commodity of God.[13]

---

[13] Charters, *Newspaper*, 1.

The proclamation of the universal reign of God, as David Bosch has indicated, transforms mission into social and political ethics,[14] or what is sometimes called the construction of an appropriate public theology.[15] Walter Brueggemann makes fundamentally the same point when he notes that the kingdom of God is the core metaphor for the creation of a new social imagination.[16] In practical terms, this is to make clear that the gospel is fundamentally concerned with all that leads to the flourishing of human life and is diametrically opposed to all that leads to the distortion and diminution of human life. That can only mean that the church in each community represents those who are there to work for the shalom of that community. In that sense, there is no distinction between the clergy and the laity, instead all are public servants committed to policies and programmes that bring about reconciliation, justice and liberation and so contribute something to 'the common good'.[17]

The Recovery of the Bible as Scripture

If modernity has successfully marginalised the church, it has also effectively closed the Bible. Recent research by the British and Foreign Bible Society shows that 18% of regular churchgoers have never read anything in the Bible for themselves. An additional 14% have not read anything from the Bible in the last year. Adding both figures together, we have the startling and disturbing statistic of 32% of regular churchgoers with no habit of Bible reading at all! This is symptomatic of a deeper malaise.[18]

Scripture is not just an amalgam of different genres of literature. It remembers and retells the central drama of the Judaeo-Christian faith. It is the story of God's persevering love for and interaction with the creation. That story, along with the values and attitudes it inculcates in us, is no longer known to the public, nor part of the

---

[14] Bosch, *Believing*, 33–35.
[15] Himes and Himes, *Fullness*, 1–28.
[16] Brueggemann, *Imagination*, 96–109.
[17] Catholic Bishops' Conference of England and Wales, *Common*.
[18] Georgiou, *Research*.

public debate about the kind of society we wish to endorse or create. The Bible is closed both in the church and society.

One reason for the lack on interest in the Bible has been the assertion that historical-critical methods offer the only reliable means of assessing the original meaning and intent of Scripture. While this method has brought immense benefits and rewards in terms of our appreciation of the historical and cultural background to Scripture, it has also created two undesirable side-effects. One is that the Bible has increasingly become a book for a small coterie of the academic elite who are now assumed to hold the key to the real meaning and significance of Scripture, as evidenced by the media interest and hype surrounding those involved in the controversial Jesus Seminar in the USA. Another side-effect is that the analysing and dissecting of the Bible into its constituent parts, valuable and important as this is, has tended to lead to a situation where we have lost the overall plot. The 'big picture', the metanarrative of Scripture, is obscured and the overall intention of the Bible understood as scripture, which is to introduce us to the central events and characters of the story, is again subverted.

This situation has also contributed to the demise of preaching as a means of communicating the relevance and importance of Scripture to issues of public concern. Increasingly, preaching has ceased to be valued both inside and outside the church and Christians have been left without the gift of prophetic imagination whereby we are able to relate Christian faith to the social, cultural and political circumstances that pertain in our society. There is no longer any point in claiming the authority of Scripture as if that in itself is capable of convincing the general public. That authority, credibility and relevance will only be demonstrated in the critical interaction that takes place between those who convincingly apply its insights and wisdom to the problems and issues that dominate our public life.

A final reason for the decline of Bible reading is the difficulty people brought up in a non-book culture experience in reading and understanding an ancient text. Increasingly, people struggle with issues to do with textuality, interpretation and application to the world as we know it.

How then can we recover the Bible as scripture? One way is simply to let the story permeate our lives by seeing ourselves as part of the continuing drama and relating ourselves to the central aspects

of the overall plot. If we have done this, we will not be speechless or
dumb in the face of complex and apparently insoluble issues when
we open the book in the public domain. When we understand and
identify with the primary purposes of the biblical narrative and realise the import and enduring significance of its various subplots, we
become again the people of the book. This is at least part of what
Lesslie Newbigin meant when he claimed that the Christian
community is the best hermeneutic of the gospel.[19] Another crucial
factor is to realise that the Scriptures cannot be simply reduced to a
text, they are a witness to a multimedia event that should be performed as such in the public life of our society. In this way we are
able to see that

> Christian interpretation of the Bible as in some sense the constitution
> of the church is a full-time affair – in spatial terms . . . the stage on
> which the meaning of scripture is 'played out' is the public domain of
> human sociability, and that the actors in this drama are (potentially) all
> of us.[20]

The Re-enchantment of the World

Modernity set out to make the world of nature and creation accessi-
ble to us by the use of reason alone, untrammelled by reference to
extraneous authorities like tradition and the church. This confidence in the power of human reason has led to what Jürgen
Moltmann calls 'the scientific and technological project of the
modern world'.[21] We are presently scrutinising the galaxies for
evidence of black holes and developing the capability to clone
human beings. In the process, however, we have created a situation
that sociologists sometimes refer to as the 'disenchantment of the
modern world'.[22]

We have reduced the world to a place governed by impersonal
and apparently inviolable scientific laws; we have changed our
environment into a mess of sprawling cities and urban decay; we

---

[19] Newbigin, *Gospel*, 222–233.
[20] Barton, *Performance*, 8.
[21] Moltmann, *Way*, 63.
[22] For a discussion see Adorno and Horkheimer, *Dialectic*, vol. 2.

have eliminated species after species of animal and plant life; we have created ecological no-go areas and left a huge legacy of nuclear waste for future generations to cope with. In the process we have dislocated ourselves from the world of nature, we have lost our sense of being at home in the world and our capacity to wonder. We have created the phenomena of the homeless mind: profound senses of alienation and anomie. In the words of one theologian, we have turned the world into a giant supermarket where 'absent-mindedly yet at the same time absorbed in what we are doing, we push our shopping carts up one aisle and down the other, while death and alienation have the run of the place.'[23]

In seeking to dethrone science from its place of power and control, some of the advocates of postmodernity are simply revelling in irrationality, while others are seeking a re-enchantment of the world. With this latter group we can join forces as we once again declare to the homeless strangers of the modern era that we stand under a firmament of truth and greatness and indeed the heavens declare the greatness of God (Ps. 19). The world is not a place of emptiness where all we can do is inoculate ourselves against the prevailing culture of despair, but is full of the mysteries of faith and the purposes of God. It is those mysteries of faith that we celebrate in Christian worship, a vision of wholeness, a liturgical re-enactment of the whole council of God. The renewal of the creative energy and symbolic power of Christian worship should not be based simply on the need for liturgical innovation or the desire to accommodate different tastes. It should be the arena where faith is renewed, our love of God and each other refocused, and the world re-enchanted. Otherwise we will be left isolated and alienated in the type of world described by Michael Polanyi:

Law is no more than what the courts will decide, art but the emollient of nerves, morality but a convention, tradition but an inertia, God but a psychological necessity. Then man dominates a world in which he himself does not exist. For with his obligations he has lost his voice and his hope, and has been left behind meaningless to himself.[24]

---

[23] Soelle, *Death*, 8.
[24] Polanyi, *Knowledge*, 380.

The Reinvention of the Human Person

Postmodernism is sometimes referred to as post–ideological. It is the product of a period of recent history that has witnessed not just the decline of organised religion but the decline of the Grand Ideologies: national socialism, fascism, Marxism, totalitarian communism. Such ideologies established themselves as counter-religions that upheld a particular view of human nature and our relation to the world. For Marx, liberation was freedom from economic alienation and would be brought about by social revolution. The apparent failure of Marxism undermined the philosophical cogency of its attempt to redefine the nature of the human person.

Advocates of modernity offer many other alternative definitions of what it means to be human. Devotees of modern science, for example, declare that we are the chance product of an evolutionary cocktail that has produced a rather sophisticated animal, driven by a selfish gene and therefore likely to create misery unless checked by the powers of the state and the judiciary. Psychoanalysts, on the other hand, claim that we are terrorised by dark subterranean forces in the human psyche that create all sorts of false and unrealisable expectations. Biologists suggest that the more we unravel the DNA code, the more we find that we are simply determined by the coded information we inherited from our family tree. Consequently moral categories such as freedom, justice and responsibility are an illusion.

For many in contemporary culture, even after two hundred years of secular humanism, it is not at all obvious what it means to celebrate our common humanity. Consequently the Grand Ideologies have been replaced by 'soft ideologies' such as the free market, the American way of life or New Age utopianism.[25] As Lakeland puts it:

> The postmodern human being wants a lot but expects little. The emotional range is narrow, between mild depression at one end and whimsical insouciance at the other. Postmodern heroes and heroines are safe, so far beyond that we could not possibly emulate them,

---

[25] Bosch, *Believing*, 47–53.

avatars of power or success of money or sex – all without consequences. . . . Postmodernity may be tragic, but its denizens are unable
to recognize tragedy. The shows we watch, the movies we see, the
music we hear, all are devoted to a counterfactual presentation of life
as comic, sentimental and comfortable.[26]

If the church is to address this conundrum, we must be clear that our
churches are not primarily hospitals for the spiritually insane, or
sanctuaries for the emotionally disturbed, or refuges for the battered
and bruised, but centres of pilgrimage and exploration where we
seek to discover what it means to be a human being.

The Christian faith claims that we are made in the image of our
Creator but have been fractured and dislocated from our true purpose by the powers of sin and evil, that also reside in this world, but
from which we can be healed and liberated through faith in Jesus
Christ. This liberation of course involves us, like Jesus, in a great
personal struggle and commitment to the cause of social justice, for
the reason he came and lived and died amongst us was to reveal to us
the nature of true humanity and so to remake and refashion us in his
own image. The good news of the gospel is that the reinvention of
the human person is an eschatological reality. It is both here and not
yet here. However, it can be anticipated and discovered in the community of the church. But the reorientation of our churches into
pilgrimage communities characterised by true humanity will not
happen easily or overnight. In fact the reverse is likely to be the case.

One overhears much talk in some sections of the church about
the need for and impending probability of revival. A brief study of
church history and an honest appraisal of one's own spiritual journey reveals that revivals are usually proceeded by a wilderness
experience. It is in the desert that we face our own vulnerability,
isolation and despair. It is the transforming reality of this disloca-
tion of ourselves and our churches from the prevailing models of
success and the triumphalism of easy-believism that will give us the
courage and prophetic insight to face the future with hope and
integrity. It is just such a situation that a contemporary prophet in
our midst recognises:

---

[26] Lakeland, *Postmodernity*, 8–9.

The Churches in Britain on the whole are not marginal, not poor, not desperate. They hold a very privileged position, their voices are heard (though there is a selective deafness). But this situation is probably ending, and Churches are likely to become more marginal. They will need to earn the right to be heard by the intrinsic sense of what they say, and by their own integrity and credibility. This could be the salvation of the Churches, but we will need to develop new and far stronger forms of solidarity and sustenance. We are probably entering a new desert period, a dark time, in which our own ability to cope with despair and desolation will be tested and purified.[27]

Bibliography

Adorno, T. and M. Horkheimer, *Dialectic of Enlightenment*, Vol. 2 trans. J. Cumming (London: Verso, 1986)

Barton, C. S., 'What a Performance' in *The Bible in Transmission: A Forum for Change in Church and Culture* (Swindon: British and Foreign Bible Society, 1998)

Berger, P. L., *The Heretical Imperative: Contemporary Possibilities of Religious Affirmation* (New York: Anchor, 1979)

—, *The Sacred Canopy: Elements of a Sociological Theory of Religion* (New York: Doubleday, 1967)

Bosch, D., *Believing in the Future: Toward a Missiology of Western Culture* (Pennsylvania: Trinity Press International, 1995)

—, *Transforming Mission* (New York: Orbis, 1991)

Brueggemann, W., *The Prophetic Imagination* (Philadelphia: Fortress, 1978)

Catholic Bishops Conference of England and Wales. *The Common Good and the Catholic Church's Social Teaching: A Statement* (London: The Catholic Bishops Conference of England and Wales, 1996)

Charters, R., in *The Church of England Newspaper* No. 5407, April 17 (1998), 5

Fiorenza, S. E., *In Memory of Her* (London: SCM, 1983)

Fung, R., *The Isaiah Agenda* (Geneva: Risk Book Series, 1992)

---

[27] Leech, *Sky*, 108.

Gates, J., *The Ownership Solution* (London: Penguin, 1998)

Georgiou, G., *Bible Society Research* (Swindon: British and Foreign Bible Society, May 1997)

Hauerwas, S. and H. W. Willimon, *Resident Aliens* (Nashville: Abingdon, 1989)

Himes, J. M. and R. K. Himes, *Fullness of Faith: The Public Significance of Theology* (New York: Paulist Press, 1993)

Lakeland, P., *Postmodernity: Christian Identity in a Fragmented Age* (Minneapolis: Fortress, 1997)

Leech, K., *The Sky is Red: Discerning the Signs of the Times* (London: Darton Longman & Todd, 1997)

Moltmann, J., *The Way of Jesus Christ: Christology in Messianic Dimensions* (London: SCM, 1990)

Newbigin, L., *The Gospel in a Pluralist Society* (London: SPCK, 1989)

—, *Foolishness to the Greeks: The Gospel and Western Culture* (London: SPCK, 1986)

Polanyi, M., *Personal Knowledge: Towards a Post-Critical Philosophy* (Chicago: University of Chicago Press, 1958)

Schleiermacher, F., *On Religion: Speeches to Its Cultured Despisers* (New York: Harper Torch Books, 1958)

Shenk, W., 'Mission, Renewal and the Future of the Church', *International Bulletin of Missiological Research* 21.4 (1997),154–9

Soelle, D., *Death by Bread Alone: Texts and Reflections on Religious Experience* (Philadelphia: Fortress, 1978)

Wink, W., *The Powers That Be* (New York: Doubleday, 1998)

Winter, B. W., *Seek the Welfare of the City* (Carlisle: Paternoster, 1994)

3

The Old Testament and the Enjoyment of Wealth

J. Gordon McConville

The Goodness of Creation

Yahweh who delivered Israel from Egypt is God who created the world. To put it differently, the horizon of the Old Testament is creation, not just redemption.[1] The Old Testament is not exclusively interested in the special story of ancient Israel, but in the whole world. In scholarly writing about the Old Testament, this could not always be taken for granted. It was thought that Israel's experience of God who acted in history to redeem his people (from slavery in Egypt) stood in contrast to the fertility gods of the other ancient peoples, who controlled the life forces of the earth. Such an opposition is now recognised as false. Indeed it is essential to hold together the two dimensions of God's activity, not only his purpose to save, but also his purpose in and for everything he has made. The wariness of a creation theology on the part of older critics arose from a fear that a 'creation' god alone might become identified with power, either to justify some political ideology or to harness the

---

[1] This point is elaborated by Brueggemann, *Theology*, 159–64. The older view could be found in von Rad, 'Problem'; cf. his *Theology* vol. I, 418–59. It persists in certain interpretations of the Wisdom literature, where Wisdom traditions, as a common coin of the ancient world, and often associated with creation theology, are thought to offer a deliberate alternative to covenantal ones; see Crenshaw, *Wisdom*, 190. For further bibliography and critique, see Van Leeuwen, 'Proverbs', 26–27.

potential in the world without reference to ethical standards.[2] And there has been reticence in some quarters because of a suspicion that the Old Testament's 'worldly' spirituality stood in some tension with the heavenly-mindedness of the New.

In the Old Testament, however, the power of the God of creation is at the service of his purpose to procure deliverance, community and justice. This purpose underlies the story of the covenant with Israel, which in turn points towards the salvation of the world. This means that we must consider, not just that the Old Testament has a full-blooded view of life, but how this attitude relates to what is right and just. In the minds of the biblical writers, the 'goodness' of the created world finds a regular echo in the 'goodness' of right relationships and behaviour. The enjoyment of the good life cannot be separated from the knowledge and service of God who gave it.

The Old Testament portrays the enjoyment of the good things of creation in positive, even lyrical, terms. It begins more or less on page one (Gen. 1) with the creation of a world that God pronounces 'good', and the gift of its riches to the human beings (Gen. 1:29–30). '*Adam*, the human being, is made from '*adamah*, the ground, hinting at the outset that human life will be lived in an inescapable dependence on the earth. And the unfolding story of Genesis has a good deal to do with food and drink! – from the first trifling with the garden's dessert menu (Gen. 3:1–7), to Noah's sampling of the vine (Gen. 9:20–21), Abram's ceding of the rich Jordan valley to nephew Lot (Gen. 13:9–10), his feeding of the mysterious divine visitors (Gen. 18:6–8), and Joseph's provision for famine-struck Egypt (Gen. 41). Blessing, indeed, often seems to be summed up in solidly material and physical terms: Jacob's blessing of his son Judah, its messianic overtones notwithstanding, is a case in point (Gen. 49:8–12).

And it is not only Genesis that holds out an Edenic ideal; it lies behind much of the Old Testament. The story of Israel's earliest days has mouth-watering images of the 'promised land' of Canaan (Exod. 3:17, cf. 23:25–26; Deut. 8:7–10). Indeed, the symbol of the promised land as a giant bunch of grapes borne along by the Israelite spies (Num. 13:23) has had lasting potency, as the Israeli Tourist

---

[2] Brueggemann, *Theology*, 163.

Board well knows! The Wisdom literature, too, understands the blessing of God as the full range of the good things of creation (e.g. Prov. 10:3–5; 31:10–31). The Psalmists trust and praise God for providing all that is needed for a full life (Ps. 104:14–15; 128; 144:12–14; 145:15–16). And the prophets, when they have finished castigating wayward Israel, hold out the prospect of a rich restoration to the fruitfulness of the land (Is. 49:8–10; Ezek. 36:8–11). Land, indeed, is a potent symbol in the Old Testament. It is much more than merely an area subject to political aspiration and dispute; rather, it is the means of life. And the promise of land speaks of God's purpose to give and sustain life, not just at some minimum level, but so that the good creation may be richly experienced. Long life, many children, red meat with good wine, bread and sweet things – for the Old Testament writers these are the ingredients of a happy life. In this embrace of the world, they are not much different from their ancient neighbours, preoccupied as they were with the perpetual counterpoint of life and wealth, lack and death, a dialectic engraved even in the geography of both Egypt and Palestine.

Wealth in Its Place

Our concern, then, is to think through the ways in which the Old Testament's realism about human life is, and may be, morally comprehended.[3] It is plain even from that first fateful decision in Eden

---

[3] This article assumes that it is legitimate to use the Old Testament as a resource for theological and ethical questions. The theoretical justification for this approach is the concept that, as well as pointing prophetically to Christ, the Old Testament has a 'surplus', that is, a range of matters about which it speaks distinctively within the context of the whole biblical canon. The term is taken from Miskotte, *Gods*, 173–302, where he expounds this idea. A modern exponent of biblical theology is Brueggemann who writes of the 'density' of the Old Testament text, namely its capacity to speak on many matters in different and ever-new ways (*Theology*, 55f.); he exemplifies this, on a subject close to the present one, in his *Land*. We cannot discuss further here the question of the relationship between Old Testament and New Testament spirituality in relation to wealth; but see the essay of Thorsten Moritz in the present volume.

that consumption of the good things of the world is bound up with matters of right and wrong, relationships with God and with fellow creatures. To put the question more broadly, how can there be a right relationship between human beings and the things that may be desirable in the world? – or better, between human beings, earth with its created things, and God? This triangle underlies the Old Testament's thinking about creation. If Eden is innocent enjoyment of the good garden, it is so because there is harmony between the man and the woman, between them and the other creatures, and between them and God. And the harmony is not merely an absence of enmity or competition, but an actual interdependence, a being there for the other. The humans are to 'work' the ground, to enable it to produce what it can (Gen. 2:5); the ground in turn brings forth fruit (2:9); the woman is to be a 'help' to the man (2:18, implying no inferiority, but rather a complementary equality). As for the harmonious relationship between the humans and God, it consists in the fact that he has 'given' the produce of the world to the humans, as indeed to the other creatures (1:29–30); that the humans bear a responsibility for the earth, at his command (1:26–28); and that their 'consumption' of the earth's bounty is limited by the condition he sets, that they should not eat 'the tree of the knowledge of good and evil' (2:17). In these harmonies lie the lineaments of the paradisal picture of Genesis.

This pattern, too, is found not just in Genesis but widely in the Old Testament. The interdependence of created things is the subject of Psalm 104, where there is a strong sense of the parts of creation being 'for' each other in the world that God has made and for which he is praised. The idea of an order that embraces both the moral life and the material world is often associated strongly with Deuteronomy, which holds out the promise of land and at the same time demands that Israel keep the terms of the covenant made at Sinai (Deuteronomy 4 provides an extended reflection on this). The theme finds its chief development in the Wisdom literature, however, with its strong interest in 'order', meaning both the harmonious relationship among the parts of the created world and the moral order of the universe, rooted in the character of God (Prov. 1:7). In the parent-child instruction of Proverbs 1–9, the learner is urged to live a life that is active and productive, and also obedient to the commandments of God. On the one hand, prosperity is secured by diligence, like that of the busy ant, while poverty will steal upon the lazy (Prov. 6:4–11); on the other hand, security and peace depend on obedience to God, while a life can be ruined by giving in to the false allure of immorality (Prov. 6:20–29).

Wealth as Problem

It will be seen immediately that the equations set up in this way lead to serious questions. Does the Bible teach that wealth and prosperity can always be expected as a result of an upright life? And does the converse follow, that a sinful life results in misery? If so, it would be untrue in experience, and therefore an impoverished doctrine and even a cruel deception. The ethics of the Wisdom traditions are sometimes characterised as a journey from relatively naive confidence (Proverbs) to developed scepticism (Ecclesiastes).[4] The former, furthermore, is also sometimes cast as 'deuteronomic', and therefore especially influential in the Old Testament.[5]

In contrast to this view, I believe it is the united witness of the Old Testament – Deuteronomy and Proverbs as well as the more overtly 'questioning' literature – that the relationship between the moral life and the enjoyment of the good things of creation cannot be taken for granted. This relationship is played out both in the drama of the Old Testament story and in the literature of worship, prophecy and Wisdom. All of these know that there is a tension between the real and the ideal in this respect. The prophets, accusing the rich of oppressing the poor, find a society in which the wicked seem to have the upper hand. Oppression takes the form of depriving fellow-Israelites of their rights to a share in the land (e.g. Is. 5:8–10).[6] The historical narratives sound the same theme, for example, when King Ahab uses his power to grab the vineyard of innocent Naboth, killing him in order to get it (1 Kgs. 21). The situation in Deuteronomy itself is more subtle, but the book acknowledges the problem in the following way: in its portrayal of

---

[4] For example Crenshaw, *Wisdom*, 126.
[5] Affinities between Proverbs and Deuteronomy have been stressed by Weinfeld, *Deuteronomy*, 244–81.
[6] See Davies, *Prophecy*, 65–89.

God's expulsion of the Canaanite peoples from the promised land and his gift of the land to Israel, it suggests that the theme of the nations' punishment for their sins should find its counterpart in a story of Israel's righteousness. Instead, Deuteronomy shows forcefully that Israel possesses no such righteousness, but rather is deeply and habitually sinful (Deut. 9:4–6). The good land is occupied by a people that is no better than those who were driven out of it because of their sins! Israel's loss of the land in due course is a consequence of its failure to keep the covenant; yet that failure seems inevitable given the nation's imperfect moral character. Israel's ultimate restoration can only be by an act of grace (Deut. 30:1–10). The imbalance between the qualification (innocence or righteousness) and the consequence (the blessings of land) is resolved in a way that might be called eschatological. Deuteronomy sets out its strong exhortations to right behaviour in the life of the here and now in full knowledge that a final convergence of righteousness and blessing can only happen as the result of a new act of God in a future time. It is therefore entirely played out in a tension between the real and the ideal. The historical books that follow Deuteronomy (Joshua to Kings), widely regarded as exhibiting a 'deuteronomic' theology, also refuse to assert a match in present time between righteousness and blessing (as the story of Ahab and Naboth shows), but finish on a note that leads into a future that is unknown (2 Kgs. 25) and simply trust that God will act mercifully, come what may.[7]

Nor does Proverbs oversimplify the relationship between righteousness and blessing. Van Leeuwen has shown that Proverbs is only properly understood when read as a *book*. That means that its meaning should not be falsely derived from individual sayings, or particular types of sayings; rather, the various sayings should be allowed to stand alongside each other in mutual qualification. Then a highly nuanced view of life emerges, in which the connection between righteousness and blessing is taken to be in principle right and expected, but is often not realised in practice. Proverbs that express this dissonance between what is expected and what actually happens include those with the pattern: 'Better . . . than . . .' (e.g.

---

[7] Provan, *Kings*, 279–81 and, slightly differently, the present writer, 'Narrative', 47–48.

Prov. 15:16–17; 16:16, 19), which acknowledge that the righteous and the wise do not always live in ideal situations.[8] Here too, the resolution of the tension between expectation and experience is deferred to an indefinite future. Finally, recent works on the Psalms have shown that there, too, the praise of God is adopted by the faithful in spite of present experience and in faith that God will establish justice in the end.[9]

These observations show that no part of the Old Testament asserts the connection between righteousness and blessing in a crude way. Answers to the problem of experienced injustice are varied. For the psalmist, the proud, successful wicked live dangerously (Ps. 73:18–20). The prophets sometimes show that feverish gain brings only hollow rewards (Is. 5:10; Hag. 1:6). In general, however, the books of the Old Testament look for the realisation of the moral harmonies only in a future time. One effect of this pattern in the Old Testament is to assert God's freedom in relation to the things he has made, and to obviate any false belief in human power to exercise final control over forces inherent in the material world.

The Good Things of Creation: Recovering a Right Perspective

We have now cleared some ground for a proper evaluation of the Old Testament's attitude to the good things of creation and our enjoyment of them. Because of the created order articulated in many parts of the Old Testament, wealth can be enjoyed when it is acknowledged as God's gift, and when it finds its proper place in the context of healthy relationships. The theme can be pursued by considering a number of topics: (1) land, (2) commandments and laws, and (3) sacrifice.

Land

Land, as we have already noted, is one of the powerful ideas of the Old Testament, an important presupposition of all Old Testament

---

[8] Van Leeuwen, 'Wealth'.
[9] See Creach, 'Shape'; Zenger, 'Composition'.

theology. It is at the heart of all its chief themes and modes: creation, exodus, covenant, law, worship, Wisdom. All are played out between the opposite possibilities of possessing and not possessing. The creation stories (Gen. 1–2) place human beings in the context of a sustaining earth. Land as productive soil and land as living space are never wholly distinguished from each other (each of the 'land' words, *'erets* and *'adamah*, can carry either sense, depending on context). The patriarchal blessings frequently revolve round the idea of plenty (Gen. 49:14–15, 22–26). The paradigm story of the Old Testament, the Exodus narrative, relates what is essentially the movement of Israel from slavery in the land of another people to possession of a land of their own. Descriptions of the bounty of the land are at the heart of the covenantal promise to the people and are couched in extravagant terms (Deut. 6:10–12; 8:7–10; 11:9–12). The pentateuchal laws have as a guiding principle the need to ensure the security of every family and individual in the commonwealth. Worship honours the God who has given land by bringing him land-borne gifts (Deut. 12). And Wisdom shows how the wise can live productively in their environment.

Let us look more carefully at the way in which the land theme functions. The close relationship between land, people and God, as it emerges from the pentateuchal laws and the narratives that follow, has been perceptively described by C. J. H. Wright.[10] The essence of the pattern is to put human life in the context of relationships, rights and duties. All behaviour is constrained by the fact that God is the giver of life itself, and of a framework in which to live it. This framework is physical (land) and social (the people of Israel in its tribes, clans and extended families). Israelites are not 'islands', but live in mutual dependence. Land (which can be extended to mean all wealth) is basically God's (Lev. 25:23), distributed to Israel as gift, or 'inheritance' (Deut. 4:20–21) in such a way as to avoid excessive accumulations and inequities. The idea of land as inheritance is defined in relation to family and clan, securing both dimensions of divine gift and familial belonging. This is the concept that lay behind Naboth's refusal to countenance Ahab's bid for his vineyard, and why the king's seizure of it by another kind of right, that of

---

[10] C. J. H. Wright, *People*, 71–114, especially 104–14.

royal prerogative and might, was so great an offence in the eyes of the biblical writer (1 Kgs. 21). The social theory of ancient Israel is not just an accidental moment in the history of social organisation, but expresses something profound about regulating human entitlement to the things of creation. The enjoyment of wealth, properly practised, is thus an essential part of human life and well-being.

Commandments and laws

The point may be taken further by noticing the role of the commandments and other laws in relation to land. The ten commandments themselves are not an abstract code of ethics, but are a kind of charter for the life of the people who have been brought out of Egypt; hence the introduction in which God recalls that event (Exod. 20:1). They are the basis of a free society as opposed to an enslaved people. The freedom depends on two factors. The first is an acknowledgement of God who has freed them in the first place, the explicit theme of at least the first four commandments (Exod. 20:3–11). And the second lies in the kind of society that the commandments intend to secure. It is not quite accurate to divide the commandments into the God-ward (numbers 1–4) and the human-ward (numbers 5–10), as has often been done. This is because there is considerable overlap between the two, which rests in a profound connection between religion and society. The sabbath command demonstrates the link clearly. The specification that that enforced rest applies to the household, guests and even animals is not given for the sake of enforcement itself, but in order to extend the benefits of the sabbatical rest to all and sundry.

Sabbath, in fact, is one of the key ideas in our study. It is rooted in the soil. The sabbath day is the first and greatest of the feasts of Israel (Lev. 23:1–3). By its temporary abandonment of the means of production, it acknowledges that God is the giver and that true enjoyment of the things of creation depends on the recognition that they are a gift; and at the same time it levels Israelites by ensuring their participation together in worship of God and enjoyment of his rest from the anxieties of labour for food. (We shall return in a moment to the sabbatical *year*.)

The remaining commandments may all be summed up in a single idea: they permit the growth and development of the *other*. All the negatives ('thou shalt not!') turn out to be a practical doctrine of love. Prohibitions of killing or stealing are obviously fundamental to such a code. But adultery, too, is no private matter: to deprive another of wife or husband or mother or father is tantamount to depriving that person of life and the means to it. And 'false witness' is lying with a view to destroying. Finally, 'coveting', that strong craving that brings forth all the rest, shows how close the desire to consume lies to the deepest hostility to God and other people.

If the ten commandments are a kind of charter, it takes the elaborated laws of Israel to begin to work out in specific cases how these things might apply. For example, the prohibition of stealing is broadened into other laws that actively require Israelites to care for other people's needs, even at the expense of their own: they should not glean every last stalk of corn, or shake down the very last olive from the tree when they harvest, but leave some for the poor (Deut. 25:19–22).

The most far-reaching extension of the principles of the ten commandments is in the idea of jubilee (Lev. 25). It is in this context that we meet the sabbatical *year*. According to Leviticus, every seventh year the fields were not to be cultivated, but left fallow while the people depended on the produce of the previous year to feed them in this one too (the same idea is found in the story of the manna in Exodus 16:21–26). Quite apart from the agricultural benefits from such a practice (which the Israelites may or may not have known about), this requirement, like the sabbath day, both acknowledges that God is the giver of everything, miraculously if necessary (Lev. 25:21), and ensures rest, and therefore dignity, for all and sundry (Lev. 25:1–7).

The biggest party comes after seven cycles of these sabbatical years, when the sabbatical year (year forty-nine) is followed by yet another in year fifty! This is the jubilee. It is the epicentre of the Old Testament's ethics of 'having'. And it is a great healing of harms. For in this year all people are allowed to return to their ancestral property. This is such an alien thought in the modern world that it bears pausing over. People who have lost property over the years through misfortune, and perhaps have fallen into slavery, are to be released and returned to their family lands. A careful reading of Leviticus 25 reveals that here the concepts of buying and selling are much closer to our concept of leasing: property values depend on the length of time that remains until the jubilee. Those forced to sell have rights of redemption for the time when they become able to exercise them; but even if they cannot redeem their property, it will in any case revert to them in the jubilee (Lev. 25:28).

It follows that slavery also has this temporary nature, and enslavements, like property leases, are dissolved in the jubilee (Lev. 25:39–43). Indeed, slavery, far from being the ruthless thing that modern history knows, had a certain social function in Israel, to help the unfortunate through a bad time. Owners are warned to show mildness (Lev. 25:43). One slave law even envisages that a slave might choose to stay with an indulgent owner (Exod. 21:5–6; Deut. 15:16–17). The law in Deuteronomy 15:12–18, however, extends the jubilee principle, so that the period of possible enslavement should never exceed six years. It also lays a heavy requirement on the owner not merely to release the slave, his 'brother', but also to restore him and his family to a condition in which he may be self-sufficient once more.

In the same vein, Israelites must not take interest on loans from each other (Deut. 23:19–20), and debts must even be cancelled in the sabbatical cycle (Deut. 15:1–11). Items taken as security on loans must be returned if they are essential to a person's well-being (Deut. 24:10–13).

All of these laws completely reverse the strong connection between wealth and human power. The Old Testament laws were an instrument to prevent exploitation. There is no irresistibility or inevitability of economic forces here. Economic life is thoroughly life before God, and the duty to God is everywhere brought to bear against the human tendency to acquire out of greed or for the sake of acquisition alone. The genius of these laws is in expressing the lordship of Yahweh in the life of Israel. Israel's relation to the land and wealth is governed by their service of him, and therefore *not* of Pharaoh of Egypt or the lesser tyrannies of Canaan. The Exodus event issues in a life governed by laws such as these, where service of Yahweh effects a liberation from the determinism and subjugation of Egypt.[11] (Unfortunately there is little evidence that Israel ever observed these commands – Jeremiah 34:8–16 might be

---

[11] The point is well made, especially in relation to the jubilee, by Levenson, *Bible*, 145–51.

the exception that proves the rule! But their failure to live up to their calling is what the prophets were called to oppose.)

Sacrifice

If the social laws of Israel preserve the rights of Israelites to enjoy a share of the good things of creation, the sacrificial laws ensure that God is acknowledged as the giver of everything. In reality there is no clean dividing line between sacrificial and social laws, since the religious life of Israel simultaneously expressed the duty of Israelites to each other, as illustrated by the sabbath. However, it is important to understand more about the Old Testament's concept of holiness at this point.

People today probably think of holiness as a kind of moral purity and spiritual seriousness. This is not the Old Testament's primary concept (though it does occur). There holiness has more to do with a visible, tangible sphere set aside for God. It is symbolised first of all by the temple and tabernacle, and consequently by the phenomena surrounding these, namely priests, sacrifices, and the annual feasts. The people of Israel were under an obligation to honour God by worshipping him in this framework and by bringing sacrifices and offerings, which were acts of worship and which at the same time sustained the fabric and ministry of the holy place. The enduring value of such a system lies in its powerful symbolism of the fact that people's life and substance are owed entirely to God. The Old Testament's concept of holiness teaches that wealth is not purely and simply for human enjoyment, but must in some sense be handed back to God.

If this sounds all too pious, let us go on to see how the Old Testament's view of sacrifice had practical consequences. Sacrificial practice was bound into Israel's life of worship in ways that are not always evident. For example, when a worshipper brought a sacrifice in fulfilment of a vow (Lev. 7:16), it probably took place in the context of a gathering of worshippers, who in the act of worshipping are witnesses to the fulfilment of the vow. This is conveyed by a text such as Psalm 22:25: 'before those who fear you will I fulfil my vows'.

The sacrifice would have been followed by a feast (Lev. 7:16 places the vow sacrifice among those where the animal killed is

mainly consumed by the worshippers). Old Testament religion and
the sacrificial rituals at its heart are profoundly social. The most
vivid pictures of this are found in the most unexpected place: the
law code of Deuteronomy. This code requires Israelites to bring
their offerings to the place of worship, to do so as households, and to
make of them great feasts that include not only immediate family
but also the 'stranger, the orphan and the widow' – the poor and
marginalised in society (Deut. 12:11f.; 14:28f.). The social side of
religion, therefore, is more than merely developing bonds of friendship between the faithful, although that is important; it is an essential
part of the worship, actively defining and creating what society is. In
this synthesis, worship and ethics are fused; in the act of worshipping God, wealth is both brought to him and shared with those in
need (cf. Deut. 26:12–15).

The forms and content of worship profoundly express the priorities of the worshippers. There is danger in the popular half-truth
that outward forms do not matter: 'it's what is in the heart that
counts'. This can be all too comfortable, as we may never be called
to account for what is 'in the heart'. The forms of worship should
teach and reinforce concepts of God and truth, but in our attempts
to be relevant we can make them pander to our 'needs' by being
merely breezy. The picture in Deuteronomy has profound implications for the way in which the modern church expresses its
priorities through its 'rituals'. The striking thing to a modern
reader is the centralising of the marginalised. Worship events had
at their heart the declaration that God makes no distinctions
between people on grounds such as status or wealth. The Old Testament challenges the church to think through how this might
take shape in modern worship. At the simplest level, does the
worship promote the community aspect of church life? More significantly, does it affirm the lifework of all its members? This latter
is too often not well done because of a subtle preference for the
'religious' vocations, and, insidiously, for the professions that are
seen to be more honourable.

The picture in Deuteronomy is the very opposite of those
debased manifestations that led the prophets to decry the 'trampling
of God's courts' (Is. 1:12), even as people 'murdered' the poor by
oppressing them:

I (the LORD) cannot bear your evil assemblies. . . .
your hands are full of blood. . . .
seek justice, encourage the oppressed
defend the cause of the fatherless, plead the case of the widow.
(Is. 1:13–17)

The prophet might have had the deuteronomic provisions in mind in his depictions. His consumerist nightmare precisely reverses the covenantal vision; instead of a society turned outward towards God and fellow human beings, there is one turned inward, self-serving and veneered with the high-sounding sanctions of a form of religion. Any tendency in our worship to make a division between the 'religious' life and the 'real' life that people actually lead can help to make this terrible vision real.

Wealth as Possible Temptation

As we have seen, the Old Testament shows that the right enjoyment of the good things of creation is part of a whole system of relationships. It follows that failure in such relationships can bring with it a failure to relate properly to the gifts of God. The case of Ahab and Naboth has already been mentioned as an example of such abuse, where the principles of might and greed ran counter to the acknowledgement of land as God's gift and the rights of the other person. The excessive desire for wealth is an ever-present danger to its true enjoyment.

The Old Testament's most penetrating meditation on wealth as gift and as danger comes in Deuteronomy 8. We have seen that Deuteronomy contains some attractive pictures of the good things of creation (Deut. 8:7–10; 11:9–12). This chapter, however, expresses vividly the dilemma posed by these gifts. It is a sharp dilemma, because it is truly God's wish to bless his people. Yet, human nature being what it is, the very enjoyment of wealth has the capacity to obscure the memory that it comes as the gift of God. And this can have destructive consequences.

The passage that has the most wonderful evocation of bounty (Deut. 8) is therefore also the one that stresses most carefully the need for the people to remember God. The chapter begins (v. 2) with a call to *remember* the journey through the wilderness, in which God provided for the people's needs. The wilderness, in fact, makes a carefully devised contrast with the fruitful land, and is used precisely to illustrate that fact that God is the source of all good, and entirely dependable in all circumstances. The miraculous food of the wilderness, the manna, is the perfect illustration of this point (v. 3). Provided only in quantities required for immediate needs, it was exactly designed to teach and nurture faith in God (see also Exod. 16:11–35). It is in this context that we find the saying made famous by being quoted by Jesus: 'man does not live on bread alone but on every word that comes from the mouth of the LORD' (8.3b; cf. Mt. 4:4). In its context in Deuteronomy 8 this saying is part of the argument that life depends on what God gives. The phrase 'every word that comes from the mouth of the LORD' is not a reference to 'word' as a spiritual thing, opposed to the material things represented by bread. It simply means that every good thing is given by God's decision, or possibly that blessing is enjoyed when life is lived according to his commandments.[12] In addition to manna, the wilderness saw other miraculous provision in the form of indestructible clothing and limbs that could take endless punishment (8:5).

The turning point in the journey from wilderness to land is the transition from a hand-to-mouth economy to a settled one in which the element of wonder has been removed. Now there is plenty, from day to day and year to year. And the call to 'remember' gives way to warnings 'not to forget' the LORD (8:11, 14). The powerful lesson of the manna is repeated (v. 16). And the moral dimension of a true view of wealth is touched again in the idea of 'testing' in the wilderness, to see if the people had a true, humble spirit (v. 16, as v. 2). The temptation to imagined self-sufficiency is articulated in

---

[12] Jesus' interpretation of the passage (Mt. 4:4) seems to take 'word' in the 'spiritual' sense just mentioned, and there has been a tradition of interpreting him in this way. However, he too teaches that 'bread' cannot be properly acquired by any kind of self-serving calculation, and that life must be lived in absolute dependence on the one who gives it. An excellent explanation is given by Perlitt, 'Mensch'; see also Van Leeuwen, 'What'.

verse 17: 'You might say: "My power and the strength of my hands have produced this wealth for me."' The point is precisely that it is imaginary; the sense of wealth as human accomplishment pure and simple is a delusion. There is great irony here: the outcome of calling wealth 'mine' is the loss of it. A wrong view of wealth is also, in Deuteronomy's vision, closely bound up with wrong religious beliefs. The ultimate result of this mix is judgement (vv. 19–20; cf. also Hos. 8:14 for an echo of the memory theme in this passage).

Deuteronomy's warnings about 'memory' remind us how much the right use of wealth demands a proper understanding of human nature. The key to avoiding the imbalance that leads into consumerism is self-knowledge as human beings made in the image of God and taught by his commandments. Deuteronomy is the book, par excellence, of God's 'Torah', that is, training or instruction. And that training is moral. Memory is not an intellectual function in this context, but a training in de-centring the self, and thus knowing one's dependence on God.

A corresponding point emerges in the 'holiness' or sacrificial realm. It is illustrated by the tragedy of Achan and his family. The scene is Jericho. The walls have fallen down (Josh. 6), and the Israelites are celebrating their first victory over inhabitants of the land of Canaan. The taking of Jericho is a proof to Israel that God really is giving them the land as he has promised. Jericho is 'devoted to destruction'; nothing is to be left alive, and nothing is to be taken by the Israelites as spoil (6:17–19). The implication of this is that Jericho is a kind of 'sacrifice', a firstfruits of the conquest, with the spoils being given to God as a sign that he was the one who ruled here and that he had given the victory. In practice this meant that the booty should be paid into the 'treasury of the LORD', that is, the coffers of the tabernacle or temple. Achan, a member of the tribe of Judah, evidently found this hard to bear; what is the point, he may have wondered, of allowing all this wealth to be paid uselessly into the funds of the priests? Surely there would be no harm in having some of it for himself and his family? Achan gave in to the temptation of assuming that goods were just goods and for consuming – and took some of the things that were 'devoted to God' (7:1). Achan's greed, therefore, is of a special sort (not unlike that of the busy traders in Amos who were impatient of the sabbath; Amos 8:5–6). It denies that God has an interest, let alone rights, in how people live their lives and in how they dispose of their wealth. Achan would have found himself at home in a modern consumerist society. The grim story ends with the capital punishment of his whole family, who have all been 'contaminated' by contact with the forbidden objects (7:22–26).

This is not the place to try to explain the Old Testament's attitude to the Canaanites or the dreadful punishment of Achan. But Achan's sin was to rebel against the fact that the good things of creation are God's to give, and they can only be enjoyed by being received according to his ordering of all of life.

Conclusion

The Old Testament's answer to the modern consumerist culture does not lie in a flight from the good things of creation; there is no ascetic doctrine here. The paradisal pictures of the Old Testament are filled with unashamed metaphors of plenty (e.g. Is. 25:6). The issue as regards the good things of creation is not whether they are there to be enjoyed, but how. The 'how' is contained in the story of Yahweh's dealings with the world he has made. In it, Yahweh creates the world and chooses and blesses a people, at the same time calling them into relationships based on justice and mutuality, thus encouraging a positive view of the enjoyment and use of wealth for the good of all. The unity of the Creator God with Yahweh of Israel enables the Old Testament's vision to be extended to all peoples at all times. The covenant with Israel functions as a paradigm. At the same time as it stands against all pagan concepts of the world, which put the forces inherent in the world at human disposal, it promotes a vision of a society that can gratefully receive 'land' because it places supreme value on the well-being of people.

The story of Israel, which is part of the biblical metanarrative applicable to all, is based on a dynamic of interaction between God and people: God blesses people, people enjoy the benefits of 'land', people worship and serve God, God goes on blessing. In this dynamic, God is always the initiator and giver, and once it is established there is no necessary end-point. Rather, the covenant is a perpetual now – 'today'; God has given-gives-will give, and this past-present-future has a deep unity. The narrative is based on promise, not an eternal projection into an ever-receding future, but rooted in memory of something already accomplished: you were slaves in Egypt. God led you out 'by a mighty hand and an outstretched arm' (Deut. 4:34). The promised 'good land' is present and future reality, simply to be enjoyed by a covenant people that perpetually renews its commitment to obedience.

Consumption of the good things of creation is a function of these core values: a people serving God and each other, receiving his blessing, and not looking to its own power to acquire. There is no question of a 'prosperity theology' here, in which possession of wealth is interpreted as God's favour for a life well lived, while poverty spells the converse. Rather, human beings are defined, given identity, by belonging to the covenant society in terms of both secure relationships and secure participation in wealth. The poor, rather than being excluded by definition from identity and belonging, are (by definition) included; their entitlement comes from their belonging, rather than their belonging from their (self-acquired) entitlement. There is a prophetic edge to the dynamic.

It is no accident that the Old Testament's vision of the use of wealth is inseparable from its vision of a healthy society. If everything in modern society is capable of being exchanged, everything in the Old Testament's social vision resists this: family remains family, land remains land (hence Naboth's revulsion at Ahab's aggressive consumerism). People may not be reduced permanently to slave status, but must be restored to the *status quo ante*: this last is the only recognised form of social development – restoration of what truly belongs.

All this stands firmly against a culture in which profit is the decisive motive. It is true that the market economy has brought prosperity to many people. The establishment of industries in poorer regions has tremendous importance for employment and thus a share in the communal wealth for those who obtain the jobs. Yet the market has casualties too, where people are outbidden for the very things they have produced themselves, or where their particular product no longer competes on world markets. 'Wealth creation' is two edged when it trades the future, or some distant part of the globe, for the immediate good. As an end in itself, it is not far from the priorities of Amos's sabbath-traders or Ahab's contempt for patrimony. The ideal of wealth creation should never be disembodied. There is no room in the biblical view for some greater economic good that sidelines actual communities. The idea of a 'trickle-down' effect falls far short of a biblical view of humanity. The result of these grand scenarios is to dehumanize all concerned, not only the underclasses that they create, but also the exploiters, like the property magnates of Isaiah 5:8.

The enjoyment of the good things of creation is God's purpose for all humanity; this much is clear from the first chapter of the Bible, and nothing else contradicts the point. In that case, actual enjoyment of them is in itself a 'good'. The temptation of consumerism is a permanent possibility in the relationship between '*adam* and '*adamah*, and not merely a characteristic propensity of the present age. The challenge to the church is to adopt the biblical paradigm of Israel, refusing to turn the truth of God's intended blessing into complacency in wealth. Where God has blessed richly, let him be blessed in turn. Where his name is taken on the lips let him be truly known as the one who has given, who still has owner's rights, and who requires a life orientated to justice and righteousness.

Bibliography

Brueggemann, W., *Theology of the Old Testament* (Minneapolis: Fortress, 1997)

—, *The Land: Place as Gift, Promise and Challenge in the Biblical Faith* (Minneapolis: Fortress, 1977)

Creach, J., 'The Shape of Book Four of the Psalter and the Shape of Second Isaiah', *Journal for the Study of the Old Testament* 80 (1998), 63–76

Crenshaw, J. L., *Old Testament Wisdom: An Introduction* (London: SCM, 1982)

Davies, E. W., *Prophecy and Ethics: Isaiah and the Ethical Traditions of Israel* (Sheffield: JSOT Press, 1981)

Levenson, J. D., *The Hebrew Bible, the Old Testament and Historical Criticism* (Louisville: Westminster/John Knox Press, 1993)

McConville, J. G., 'Narrative and Meaning in the Books of Kings', *Biblica* 70 (1989), 31–49

Miskotte, K., *When the Gods Are Silent* (London: Collins, 1967)

Perlitt, L., 'Wovon der Mensch lebt (Dtn 8,3b)' in J. Jeremias and L. Perlitt (eds.), *Die Botschaft und die Boten* (Neukirchen: Neukirchener Verlag, 1981), 403–26

Provan, I., *1 and 2 Kings* (Carlisle: Paternoster, 1995)

Rad., G. von, 'The Theological Problem of the Old Testament Doctrine of Creation' in *The Problem of the Hexateuch and Other Essays* (London: SCM, 1984), 131–143

—, *Old Testament Theology*, vol. 1 (London: Oliver & Boyd, 1962)

Van Leeuwen, R. C., 'Proverbs' in *New Interpreter's Bible* vol. v (Nashville: Abingdon, 1997), 17–264

—, 'Wealth and Poverty: System and Contradiction in Proverbs', *Hebrew Studies* 33 (1992), 25–36

—, 'What Comes Out of God's Mouth: Theological Wordplay in Deuteronomy 8', *Catholic Biblical Quarterly* 47 (1985), 55–57

Weinfeld, M., *Deuteronomy and the Deuteronomic School* (Oxford: Clarendon, 1972)

Wright, C. J. H., *God's People in God's Land* (Grand Rapids: Eerdmans, 1990)

Zenger, E., 'The Composition and Theology of the Fifth Book of Psalms, Psalms 107–145', *JSOT* 80 (1998), 77–102

4

New Testament Voices for
an Addicted Society

Thorsten Moritz

One of the daunting aspects of a dominating worldview is that it is immensely difficult to distance oneself from it in order to evaluate it critically. That option, if it existed, would be both convenient and cosy. It would enable us to do that for which Christians are sadly so well known. That is, to make far-reaching pronouncements on the state of this evil world *as if we had nothing to do with it*. However, if a *worldview* is that which allows us to make sense of our individual story in the context of the story of the world at large, it stands to reason that any attempt to pontificate on 'it' from a distance is bound to suffer a certain loss of credibility. The fact that in this age of information technology we are bound – consciously or not – to indwell more stories than one, makes the matter of understanding and critiquing dominant worldviews more rather than less intricate.

To conclude in the light of this that we as individuals cannot be held responsible for the dominant worldview is hardly an option for those committed to the faith envisaged by Jesus. True, John's Gospel reports Jesus' teaching that his disciples 'do not belong to the world' (Jn. 15:19; 17:14, 16), but this should clearly not be misunderstood in the sense of withdrawal from the world. Quite the opposite, as the text immediately emphasises (17:15, 18): Jesus' disciples have a responsibility to go into the world and to reshape it. Paul agrees with this (1 Cor. 5:10). The order of the day is *shaping*, not *escaping*. God is committed to his creation, as the Psalmists keep reminding us.[1] Christians are therefore inevitably bound up with it (Rom. 8:18–21).[2] The question this raises in an age of consumerism is this: how should one's attitude towards the things we crave and the services society advertises be reshaped in order to reflect God's creational values? The stark alternatives appear to be an unbiblical

---

[1] One of the better known examples is Psalm 8. For a psalm that praises God as Creator, see Psalm 33. There are, of course, psalms that lament the transitory nature of human life, such as Psalm 39, but is not about anticipating the end of this physical creation.

[2] A possible objection to this statement appears to be found in 2 Peter 3:10: 'The heavens will pass away with a loud noise, and the elements will be dissolved with fire, and the earth and the works upon it will be burned up.' Cf. the similar statements in Mark 13:24–27. In response, the following needs to be said: the co-text of the first passage (especially vv. 6f.) emphasises the parallel between the envisaged event and the flood at the time of Noah. By analogy, this event does not mean the physical end of this universe (as it evidently did not in the case of the flood). The language employed should instead be understood metaphorically, that is, as other-worldly language about this world. Such use of language is usually an effort to demonstrate how this world is affected by God's reality. This is supported by the metaphorical use of similar language in the second text, particularly when we consider that the imagery used there stems from Isaiah 13:10, a text which clearly refers to the imminent *this-worldly* judgement on Babylon. The only material difference between Mark 13 and Isaiah 13 at this point is that Jesus applies this imagery of judgement to Israel herself, not Israel's adversaries. It is left to the reader to imagine how this audacious claim on his part may have contributed to his being handed over for execution. One might add, regarding 2 Peter 3, that flood imagery is also employed in this way by Jesus himself according to Luke 17:26f. Like Peter, Jesus did not expect this to result in the physical end of this world. Otherwise it would be exceedingly difficult to demonstrate the logic of the practical advice given in vv. 31–35. Such advice does not make sense if it referred to the impending invasion of Jerusalem by the Roman forces at the climax of the Jewish War (AD 66–70). By taking evasive action – rather than fighting a losing battle for the wrong nationalistic reasons and against the wrong enemy, namely Rome instead of Satan (for a detailed treatment of these matters, see Borg, *Conflict* and N. T. Wright, *Jesus*, 358–367) – the disciples not only avoid the Son of Man's judgement on Jerusalem's misguided regime, they actively demonstrate that they put their trust in Jesus rather than in the doomed city.

asceticism on the one hand or succumbing to the relentless pressures of the 'market place' on the other.

It would be anachronistic to turn to the New Testament hoping to find texts that directly engage consumerism, a much later phenomenon that owes its existence to industrialisation and the means of mass production.[3] Similarly, it would be linguistically naive to scan New Testament dictionaries for the relevant entries to provide us with a neat theological summary. Theology does not work like that, nor does responsible interpretation, especially where the primary text (in this case the New Testament) addresses concerns that arose from a culture quite different to our own. To point out this cultural gap is not to admit defeat, but to remind ourselves that it is not our task to read the New Testament as a handbook on how to deal with consumerism at the end of the second millennium. Instead we need a clear understanding of how our modern and postmodern storylines differ from those of early Christianity.[4] Only then can we ask what steps and attitudes are necessary to increase the compatibility between our lifestyles and those envisaged by Jesus and emulated (with varying degrees of success) by the early Christians.

---

[3] This is not at all to deny that it was possible in biblical antiquity to acquire luxury items and to demonstrate wealth. Both the OT prophets and Jesus show with their invectives against unrighteous wealth (a phrase borrowed from Lk. 16:9) that they felt compelled to subordinate wealth – in some cases even the right to property *per se* – to the necessary care for the less well off (e.g. Am. 5:10–12; 8:4–8; Lk. 16:19–31 to list just a few examples – others can be found in Johnson, *Sharing*, 11–29 as well as in Gordon McConville's chapter in this volume). Wealth and oppression were realities then as much as they are in today's world, but it would quite obviously be wrong to speak of widespread accumulation of mass-produced commodities for the purpose of enhancing one's role or *raison d'être* within society's narrative. Such a development is only imaginable in a cultural environment where (a) mass production and large-scale advertising are available and (b) the individual has been empowered to acquire wealth independently from family or clan. New Testament society (or societies) is better described with Malina as a 'closed limited goods society' (*World*, 82–85). See the introductory essay to this volume for further discussion of the relationship between consumerism and industrialisation.

[4] For an analysis of the former, see Alan Storkey's contribution in this volume.

Despite some overlap between our experience and that of early Christian times, the challenges and the opportunities faced by the first Christians were significantly different from the ones we are considering today. For instance, they had little if any hope of impacting their Graeco-Roman environment by affecting legislation. The Roman Empire was quite simply not that type of place, neither politically nor in terms of the power wielded by local cults. Today it is at least conceivable – and occasionally it does happen – that a Christian lobby succeeds in persuading a Member of Parliament to propose fresh legislation, even if only in Britain by means of Parliament's 'ten-minute rule'. Such political lobbying is not only desirable but essential – it would be inexcusable to play down its significance. Having said that, in view of the pervasive nature of the consumerist worldview it would be illusory to think that the main burden of responsibility for reshaping society's values can be shouldered by Christian lobbying groups and the legislature. Such lobbying needs to be underpinned by Christian practice at grass-roots level, and that for at least two reasons: First, in a democracy it is from this level that lobbying groups derive their continuing mandate. Secondly, if it is a mark of God's people to 'seek the welfare of the city' (Jer. 29:7; cf. Phil. 1:27–2:18; Rom. 13:1–7; Gal. 6:9f.), the Christian imperative to embody Christ's values (Eph. 5:1f; Phil. 2:5–8) must not be restricted to only some spheres of life or layers of society.

Our task in this chapter is analytical, not merely descriptive. We are primarily looking for theological bedrock on which to reflect about today's world, not straightforward ethical prescription that translates seamlessly. Unless we are keenly aware of the need to read the texts contextually, we will be driven to conclude that the relevant evidence in the New Testament appears rather inconsistent. Should we leave any notion of material prosperity behind (Lk. 5:28)? Should we give away half of our possessions to the poor (Lk. 19:8), or even all (Lk. 18:22), or more than we can realistically afford (Mk. 12:44; 2. Cor. 8:1–4)? Should we have all things in common (Acts 2:41f.; 4:32)?[5] Should we retain some wealth for

---

[5]   This ideal has interesting parallels in various Greek traditions that predate Christianity and are reflected in a variety of Greek proverbs (cited in Aristotle, Plato and a number of biographies of Pythagoras – see Johnson, *Sharing*, 119, 140 for details). Johnson emphasises that in these traditions

now in order to assist poor fellow Christians in times of famine
(Jn. 13:29; Acts 9:27–30)?[6] Can God's people expect an increase in
material wealth such as cattle, silver and gold (Gen. 12:16; 13:2)?
After all, 'everything God created is good . . . if it is received with
thanksgiving' (1 Tim. 4:4). Is the accumulation of wealth legitimate
as long as we retain with Job the ability to say 'blessed be the name of
the Lord', having seen our possessions disappear? Even this cursory
and slightly facetious glance at some of the biblical evidence suggests
that this issue cannot be one of hard and fast rules. Christian living
has a great deal more to do with making sense of our personal *and
social* stories in the light of God's bigger picture for his people and
creation than it does with observing a set of rules and regulations.

How can we best account for the genuine diversity of the evidence? What does it mean to look for 'theological bedrock'? Is there
an underlying 'canonical' unity of these texts? If there is, how can it
be reappropriated for our own setting in a way that authentically
reflects the teaching of the New Testament? We will have to make
due allowance for the significant shifts in social behaviour and
responsibilities between the early Christian culture and our own
without, in the process, sacrificing the relevance of biblical revelation. We shall see that there are a variety of possible avenues at our
disposal. Before exploring them, we do well to ask how one can
move from the New Testament text to our own world without
falling into the trap of anachronistic proof-texting.

Two Thousand Years Later . . .

The variation mentioned above in the advice given in Scripture to
those who seek to reconcile the temptations of prosperity with faith

---

[5] *(continued)* 'the disposition of possessions carried considerable weight'
(119). A striking example of this is the Pythagorean community where
ranks of initiation were reflected by the degree of sharing possessions.
When a member was excommunicated, his or her departure was marked
by a 'double gift of money' to symbolise the severing of ties (Iamblichus,
Life of Pythagoras, 17:72f.).
[6] Note that the financial help depended on 'the ability of each disciple to
contribute' (v. 29). This presupposes varying degrees of personal possession
even in the early churches.

acutely reminds us that the line from any given New Testament text to our own experience is anything but straight. This can be demonstrated on a number of levels, from the simple to the more complex:

(1) While it was perfectly acceptable to Jesus for the repentant tax collector Zacchaeus to offer to give half of his possessions away to the poor (Lk. 19:8f.), to do likewise would apparently not have been good enough for the rich young man who approached Jesus (Lk. 18:22). If nothing else, this tells us that even in earliest Christianity it would have been impossible to devise a definitive compendium of Christian behaviour. Interestingly, given that these two stories are so closely located, Luke does not seem at all concerned about the diversity of demands with which Jesus confronted these individuals.

(2) On a more complex level, it emerges that such things as the status of work and purchasing power functioned quite differently compared with today. Whereas these days it is considered quite acceptable to work with a view to enhancing one's social and economic status, this would not have been so at the time of Jesus. In those days the honourable thing to do was to regard work as a way of maintaining – not changing – one's inherited status.[7] The widely perceived problem with tax collectors, such as Zacchaeus, was not only their collaboration with the Roman oppressors but equally their attempts to be 'upwardly mobile'. The example illustrates that we must make every effort to interpret seemingly straightforward biblical stories from the perspective of a first-century Jewish worldview. In the case of the rich young man, the issue is not so acute because both then and now the resulting 'downward mobility' would have entailed a diminished social status.

(3) Supposing we had cleared the interpretative hurdles of the sort described so far, there still remains the question of authority. How can a biblical text, having been responsibly interpreted, be taken as God's authoritative voice for today's people of God? Put differently, how should we define what constitutes a theologically sound appropriation of biblical wisdom? It would be tempting at this point to appeal to the notion of 'theological principles' that we lift from the texts and reapply. So far so good, but what if a text has no intention of yielding theological principles for reapplication?

---

[7] Malina, *World*, 82f.

And even if it does, what guidance do we have for the process of reapplication? We need more than theological principles – we need a framework within which to make sense of them. The most basic framework in human experience for making sense of ourselves, others and the world around us (which is what the term 'worldview' effectively means) is that of stories.[8] In our case, the most fundamental storyline within which to make sense of theological principles is that of God's people in the world.[9] It is a story that culminates in the establishment of God's reign (or kingdom) in this world. It is for this reason that we must ask specifically about the nature of God's kingship in biblical thinking. Only then can we hope to make sense of what Jesus is reported to have taught about such things as wealth and prosperity.

The Kingdom Has Come

It is a truism in many Christian circles that according to New Testament teaching the kingdom of God is present, but not yet consummated. Scholars often refer to this tension as *inaugurated eschatology*. This is quite different from Dodd's well-known concept of *realised eschatology*, which places an exclusive emphasis on the presence of the kingdom at the time of Jesus, thus downplaying any future aspects.[10] The problem with the concept of inaugurated eschatology is that it suggests an equal balance in Jesus' teaching between present and future aspects that the evidence of the gospels does not support. While it is quite possible to demonstrate both present and imminent aspects in Jesus' kingdom proclamation,[11] those passages that have traditionally been interpreted with

---

[8] A full discussion of the role of stories for understanding the notion of worldview is provided by Wright, *People*, 38–80.
[9] Cf. Lohfink, *Kirche*, 156.
[10] Dodd, *Parables*.
[11] For the presence of the kingdom from Jesus' perspective see Mt. 12:28; 13:44–46; Mk. 2:18–22; 3:22–27; 4:21; Lk. 4:16–21; 7:18–23; 10:9–11, 23; 14:15–24; 16:16; 17:20f. The imminence of the kingdom is stressed (and sometimes requested) in the following passages: Mt. 8:11; 10:23; Mk. 1:15; 9:1; 14:25; Lk. 3:9; 11:4.

reference to the coming of the Son of Man (understood as involving the physical end of the world) prove on closer inspection to refer metaphorically to the end of the world *order* brought about by the cross. It was a theological world order that distinguished between those who were 'in' (i.e. in the covenant relationship with God) and those who were 'out' along national or ethnic lines. Its end, which Paul associates most closely with the cross (Eph. 2:13–17), was tragically symbolised by the destruction of Jerusalem by the Romans within one generation of Jesus (cf. Mk. 9:1 and 13:30). In short, it is no longer possible to use Mark 13, Matthew 13:36–43 and chapter 24, as well as Luke 17 and 21 (and much of Revelation) as evidence for the kingdom as a future entity, at least not from our post-first-century vantage point. To do so would be to fall into the trap of taking literally that which is meant to be interpreted metaphorically and expecting events in the future that actually found their fulfilment in the first century.[12]

This is not to deny, of course, that there are future components of God's kingship, even from our perspective. But, although real and important, these occupy considerably less space in Jesus' eschatology than is often assumed. There is talk of a future judgement beyond that which befell Jerusalem in AD 70.[13] Similarly there is talk of the future resurrection[14] and of the handing over of Christ's messianic kingdom to the Father.[15] But none of these important aspects of New Testament eschatology must detract attention from the thoroughly this-worldly focus of Christ's kingship claims.

The seemingly inevitable tendency in Christian preaching to place an inordinate emphasis on the future aspects is a problem insofar as it tacitly relativises the need to implement kingdom values

---

[12] In addition to Dodd, Borg and Wright, one might consult Glasson, *Jesus*, for more detailed treatments.

[13] Some would regard Luke 11:31f. and 12:8f. as falling into this category, but it is quite possible to interpret these verses in line with the interpretation of Luke 21 mentioned above, i.e. with reference to events in the first century, although admittedly this is not certain. The same applies to Mark 3:29 and Luke 10:10–15. More certain are Matthew 12:18, 36f.; 25:31–46 and John 5:22–29.

[14] Lk. 20:37; cf. Jn 6:40, 54; 1 Cor. 15:42–44; 1 Thess. 4:16.

[15] Mt. 13:41–43; cf. 1 Cor. 15:23ff. and possibly Eph. 5:5.

now. Fortunately there are numerous refreshing exceptions in the
recent history of the church in the west, such as the so-called *Kingdom Manifesto* compiled by the leaders of Te Atatu Bible Chapel in
New Zealand.[16] This Manifesto gives expression to the thoroughly
Scriptural realisation that Christ's king*ship* (probably a better translation here than 'king*dom*', a term that suggests *realm* instead of *reign*)
has a claim to implementation in *this world* and in *our cultures*. This
realisation is entirely in keeping with the manifestations of kingship
that characterised Jesus' own mission.[17] Thus we read of the reconciliation of sinners and their integration under his kingship (cf. the
numerous table-fellowship passages). We read of the release from
physical and spiritual oppression (Mk. 3:20–27; Lk. 7:18–22) and of
a new life of freedom being found (Mt. 18:10–14; Mk. 8:35–37 and
10:45). It would be tempting, though probably premature, to
contextualise this picture immediately by adding 'release from the
oppression of consumerist cravings'.

At any rate, it is clear by now that the challenge of Christ's
kingship must neither be postponed (by treating the kingdom
purely as a future entity) nor privatised (as if such matters as our
attitude towards the culture in which we live as Christians
belonged to the domain of personal piety).[18] The gospel has a claim
on society as much as it does on individuals. When Jesus sent the
disciples into the villages of Galilee (Lk. 9:1–6 and 10:1–12)
the objective was to preach *and to be* good news. In other words,
their brief was to emulate much of his own ministry. The question
therefore has to be this: what principles become operative when
God sends his people into the world to be salt and light? One of the
most fundamental principles is addressed below.

---

[16] Published in Hathaway, *Renewal*, 193–205.

[17] I am here thinking primarily of Jesus' stated objective to 'preach good
news to the poor, . . . to proclaim freedom for the prisoners, and recovery
of sight for the blind, to release the oppressed, to proclaim the year of the
Lord's favour' (Lk. 4:18f.).

[18] For a readable and very timely discussion of the enjoinders in the epis-
tles by Paul and Peter to live worthily *as citizens* (cf. Phil. 1:27), see
Winter, *Welfare*.

Kingship Implies Reversal

There are those who are last who will be first, and first who will be last (Lk. 13:30). The proverbial nature of this particular reversal saying must not blind us to the severity of what is being said here. The saying relates directly to the question of salvation. The link between this and the topic of this collection of essays may not seem immediately obvious. Yet Nickelsburg, having studied the relationship between riches and salvation in Luke and 1 Enoch, concludes that 'the accumulation and holding of riches and possessions are inversely related to the possibility of salvation.'[19] While this claim needs to be treated with caution (who are the holders of riches in this connection?), he illustrates that most of the passages about wealth and possessions occur in the context of judgement or salvation, thus demonstrating the seriousness of the matter.

As is clear from the discussion above, it would be wrong immediately to conclude that 'judgement' here means eternal judgement, or indeed that 'salvation' necessarily always means spiritual (and therefore non-physical?) restoration. To understand the force of the passages alluded to by Nickelsburg, one has to allow for the possibility that Jesus was sometimes talking about the final judgement, but sometimes about the more imminent judgement to be inflicted upon his people by means of the Romans (the so-called Jewish War AD 66–70 that culminated in the destruction of Jerusalem). This is the implication at any rate of Borg's suggestion, which I regard as essentially sound, that at the heart of Jesus' confrontation with Israel was his claim that Israel's anti-Roman agenda was misguided in the sense that her real enemy was not Rome at all.[20] Israel's real problems are not of the making of Rome at all, they are the direct result of a misguided separation paradigm, where holiness is defined in ritualistic terms rather than in terms of God's mercy,[21] thus leading to spiritual elitism on the one hand and ritualistic and social

---

[19] Nickelsburg, 'Riches', 340.

[20] Borg, *Conflict*, 145 and 213ff.

[21] Note how Jesus is portrayed as challenging the Pharisees and Scribes at least implicitly on precisely this point in Luke 5:32 and 15:1ff. (cf. 14:7–14).

segregation on the other. Such tendencies needed to be reversed and we shall see that the pronouncement of such reversals lies at the heart of Jesus' teaching.

So what is the nature of the reversals that seem so prevalent in Jesus' kingship proclamation? I will restrict this list to examples from our main source for reversals, Luke's Gospel.

1:53–55: the hungry will be filled, the rich will leave empty-handed

2:34: this child is set for the fall and the rise of many in Israel

3:4–6: valleys will be filled and mountains will be made low

6:20–26: happy are the poor, the hungry, the mourners, those hated; woe to the others

7.30–30: the sinful woman experienced redemption, the Pharisee is an ungrateful debtor

9:24: he who seeks to save his life will lose it, he who loses it will gain it

10:25–37: the good Samaritan displays neighbourly mercy, the religious leaders are incapable of that

13:30: the first will be last, the last will be first

14:7–11: those who exalt themselves will be humbled

14:12–24: the religious elite reject God's invitation, the outcasts accept it

15:1–10: the Pharisees have cause to grumble, the sinners have cause to celebrate

15:11–32: the rebellious younger son demonstrates repentance, the mature son demonstrates hardness

16:19–31: the rich man suffers anguish, poor man Lazarus dwells in comfort

17:33: he who seeks to save his life will lose it, he who loses it will gain it

18:9–14: the Pharisee will be humbled, the tax collector will be justified

18:18–30: the rich have difficulty entering the kingdom, not so those who leave everything behind

It would be difficult to avoid the conclusion that Luke wanted his audience to appropriate the reversal of injustice and idolatry as a divine principle.[22] This is neither to suggest that the reversals necessarily have a physical referent (i.e. that the rich will lose their physical wealth) – though in some cases that is true – nor that the reversal will be effected only at the end of history (final judgement). Chapter 1:53–55, for instance, refers not to financial

---

[22] York, *Last*, 182f.

wealth, but to Israel's experience in the context of political history. The same may well apply to chapter 6:20–26. Also, the redemptive experience of the sinful woman in chapter 7:36–50 has already been accomplished – hence her celebration; it is not something stored up for her to receive in the future. Those who seek to protect their lives (17:33) by engaging the Roman army, by relying on Jerusalem and by attempting to force God's hand will lose them precisely at the hands of the Romans (cf. 19:43f.), a result not unlike the fate of Lot's wife (cf. Lk. 17:32). We could extend this discussion, but that is not necessary. It is clear that Jesus envisaged reversals *in this world*. For Luke it is equally clear that the willingness to embrace reversals of values is a non-negotiable aspect of discipleship. This can be demonstrated by highlighting briefly the structure of the Lucan travel narrative (the story of Jesus' travels towards his final destiny in Jerusalem – Lk. 9:57–19:27).

The following observations emerge: there is a major section that highlights reversals in chapters 13:18–16:31. It is bracketed by two further sections on the basics of discipleship (9:57–13:21 and 17:1–19:27). These three sections taken together make up the so-called travel narrative that is the main middle section of Luke's Gospel. We see that reversals stand at the very centre of this travel narrative. The entire section is held together by a focus on spiritual and material commitment.[23] Chapters 13:18–14:35 address the need for spiritual reversals; chapter 16 the inevitability of material reversals. At its heart we find chapter 15 with its emphasis on that which is lost and which will be found. This is the core reversal in the sense that it symbolises the heart of the gospel. The arrangement of Luke's travel material could not be clearer: Jesus travels to Jerusalem to achieve the decisive reversal that leads to the finding of those who acknowledge their lostness. Some of these repentant sinners are portrayed as individuals with a dubious past. The whole point of highlighting them is precisely to illustrate the dynamic of reversal at work in the lives of those considered by many as 'hopeless cases'. Christ's kingship has the principle of the reversal of worldly values and outlooks at its very core (cf. Mk. 8:31–38) and we have to

---

[23] Cf. Lk. 12:1–53; 13:18–14:35; 16; 18:9–19:10.

understand that such reversals are needed in the lives of all, not just those who are considered to be over the edge of what society tolerates as 'normal'. Far from these things being purely private, society ought to be challenged by Christian lifestyles to learn to associate commitment to Jesus with a radical re-evaluation of material wealth. This is one of the core values of the gospel and it needs to be brought to bear on the issue of consumerism today.

Symbolism and Idolatry

What does it mean to say, as Johnson did, that we are 'living symbols of ourselves'?[24] It means, to give just one example, that we tend to express who we are or how we feel by means of our body language. More pertinently to our present topic: we tend to choose and display possessions in line with the picture of ourselves that we wish to project to others. Our accumulation and use of possessions and commodities effectively become symbols of our worldview. This is crucial in that it raises the question whether possessions are evil per se, whether they can become evil once a certain degree of wealth is achieved, or whether their moral legitimacy is contingent not so much on their monetary or status value, but on the power exercised by them over those who acquire them and the signals emanating from them to those around us. Consumerism may be a phenomenon of the 'new world',[25] rooted in early modernity, but the issue of one's attitude towards the acquisition and use of commodities as such was by no means unknown in the New Testament world. It was as normal then as it is now to use possessions for the purpose of making sense of the self in relation to society. We can therefore hope to throw light on this issue by allowing some pertinent texts to speak. I propose to divide them into two categories: (1) those that address the matter of idolatry as such, and (2) those that deal more specifically with the power and symbolism of possessions.

---

[24] Johnson, *Sharing*, 36.
[25] This is discussed in more detail in the introductory essay to this volume.

Idolatry

The Judeo-Christian faith is decidedly one of monotheism.[26] This by definition excludes idolatry. 'Idolaters are without excuse' (Rom. 1:20). Why? Because they 'exchanged the truth of God for a lie and worshipped and served created things rather than the Creator' (Rom. 1:25). Put differently, idolatry consists in the fallacy of treating the absolute as relative and vice versa. God responds by 'handing [the idolaters] over' (Rom. 1:24, 26, 28), so that they receive 'the due penalty' (Rom. 1:27). It is worth remembering that this 'handing over' is not based on something inherent in the possessions (or 'created things' – Rom. 1:23–25) held dear, but on the fact that meaning is being sought and expressed through them. It might be retorted that Paul has in mind the worship of religious artefacts, rather than the acquisition of commodities. But the underlying principle concerning the deceptive and even destructive nature of idolatry surely applies more generally. After all, Paul himself applies it only a few verses later to the issue of homosexuality (vv. 26f.) and then again to a whole range of other ethical matters (vv. 29–31).

If material idolatry results in vanity, as 'the Preacher' reminds us (Eccl. 5:9–10), the stark theological reality is that it cannot simply be counterbalanced either by personal piety in other areas of personal existence or indeed on the purely confessional level. It is pervasive in character, so much so, in fact, that it renders worthless the worship of the living God: 'These people honour me with their lips, but their hearts are far from me; they worship me in vain' (Mk. 7:6f.; cf. Is. [LXX] 29:13). The relevance of this for our topic is evident and can be expressed in the words of Colossians 3:5: 'greed is idolatry',[27] a combination of terms that is also attested in

---

[26] Ex. 20:2–5; Dt. 6:4–5; Mk. 12:29; Rom. 3:30; 10:12; 1 Cor. 8:4–6; 2 Cor. 4:5f.; Eph. 4:1–6; 1 Thess. 1:9; 1 Tim. 2:5; Heb. 6:1; Jas. 1:17f.; 1 Pet. 1:17.

[27] The term 'idolatry' only qualifies 'greed', rather than any of the other attributes mentioned in the list (sexual immorality, impurity, lust and evil desires). In 1 Timothy 6:9f. covetousness, or greed, is described in similarly harsh terms: it is 'the root of all kinds of evil', even to the point of leading to the abandoning of faith.

1 Corinthians 5:11.[28] The remedy suggested in Colossians is found
in one of the preceding verses: 'set your minds on things above, not
on earthly things' (v. 2), a piece of urgent advice[29] that echoes the
harsh words of Jesus to Peter (Mk. 8:33) after the latter displayed his
unwillingness to accept the need for Jesus' self-denial.[30] The parallel
in Ephesians 5:5 is even clearer: 'no . . . greedy person – such a man
is an idolater – has any inheritance in the kingdom of Christ and of
God.' The evident reason is that idolatry – of which material and
financial greed is a function – amounts to a *de facto* declaration that
that which is part of the material world displaces him who is the
creator of all that is in that world, including humanity.

It is not difficult to see the incompatibility between the notion
of Christ's kingship and idolatry. The former is established on the
basis of his self-denial for the benefit of others and on the principle
of this attitude being emulated by his followers (Mk. 8:31–38;
10:45; Phil. 2:5–8). The latter is to be shunned under all circumstances (1 Cor. 10:14). True wealth has been achieved and made
available to the believer by Christ, a reality that for Paul again
hinges on the principle of Christ's substitutionary self-denial

---

[28] The practical advice given in 1 Corinthians 5:11 effectively means to
withdraw fellowship from the greedy person (cf. the similar advice in Eph.
5:7). Members of the Paul Seminar (Chelmsford 1998) are agreed on the
need to discuss the cultural suitability of transferring such advice into a
modern context, but there is less agreement about how this might be
achieved.

[29] What does Col. 3:2 have in mind when it urges us to 'set [our] minds on
things above, not on earthly things'? Importantly, this is not a recipe for
escapism from this creation, but an encouragement to reassess and question our worldly values – or better, worldviews – in the light of the will of
the one who inaugurated the renewal of creation through the resurrection
of his son (v. 1). The language used at this point is obviously metaphorical
– this is abundantly clear from the following verse, which speaks of us having died (v. 3). The true life which is found in Christ (vv. 3–4) and which
is described in practical detail in chapters 3:5–4:6 is evidently not to be
lived in a sphere of transcendental otherness, but in this world and
creation.

[30] It is quite possible that Paul had this incident in mind. Cf. the following
parallels: the reference to identifying with Christ's death in v. 3 and Mk.
8:35; the glorious manifestation of Christ in v. 4 and Mk. 8:38.

(2 Cor. 8:9). To commit idolatry by craving material values is tantamount to a denial of the salvific relevance of this selfless act. If greed effectively relativises the significance of Christ's death, it cannot be tolerated on the grounds that it is a 'purely private' matter. Since it undermines the proclamation of Christ's death, it is a matter of universal soteriological concern, not personal preference.[31] To suggest therefore, that provision for the needy person within one's own community (Jas. 2:15f.) amounts to a full discharge of one's responsibility as stewards of financial and material wealth is to ignore that for James this is no more than the bare minimum that faith demands. His reasoning is precisely that one's use of possessions is indicative of one's faith commitment.

Once it is realised that the consumerist accumulation of wealth is diametrically opposed to the early Christian ethic of using possessions for alleviating the hardship of others, the difficulty of reconciling the excessive accumulation of commodities for personal consumption with the gospel emerges loud and clear. It is not only impossible to serve two masters at the same time (Lk. 16:13), it is also a better reflection of Christ's values to use one's wealth for the benefit of those needier than oneself (v. 9). If we cannot be trusted in our use of 'unrighteous mammon' (i.e. for the needy ones), how is God going to entrust us with those values that really matter (v. 11)? Paul is adamant in his second letter to the Corinthians that the Macedonian churches are exemplary in their priorities: he confirms that in the Spirit of Christ's self-denial they were happy to contribute more than they could afford to the collection for Jerusalem. Is this a paradigm that is meant for all Christians?

Possessions

On the question of the socio-economic circumstances in first-century Palestine (and especially Galilee, i.e. Jesus' main area of operation) final agreement has not yet been reached. The majority

---

[31] The social dimension of the gospel is a much ignored area in 'narrow evangelicalism'. See Winter, *Welfare* on such pertinent passages as 1 Pet. 1–2; Rom. 13:3–4; 16:23; 1 Thess. 4:11–12; 2 Thess. 3:6–13; 1 Tim. 5:3–16; Phil. 1:27–2:18; 1 Cor. 6:1–11; 7:17–24; 8:1–11:1; Gal. 6:11–18.

of scholars take the view that life was hard, especially for the owners of smallholdings and those peasants who had to pay rent to their landlords. A rather less dim view is defended by Schmidt.[32] We will return to this topic below. However, irrespective of the view one takes in regard to this question, the extent of the criticism of materialism in Judaism and the preaching of Jesus is impressive.[33] And yet it is equally clear that Jesus was brought up in a setting that could almost be described as Galilean middle class, that is, the class of skilled workers such as carpenters. The same is true for at least some of his disciples: the father of James and John employed day-labourers (Mk. 1:20); Levi, as a tax collector, would have been well off economically, albeit living a life on the fringe of society; the women who travelled with Jesus and the disciples were well-to-do (Lk. 8:1–3). Hengel reminds us that Jesus expected adult children to support their parents financially (Mk. 7:9f.), thus implying the legit-imacy of property.[34] Zacchaeus can retain a significant proportion of his possessions (Lk. 10:8f.). The list could be extended.

How can this evidence be squared with the criticism of the accu-mulation of property found in such passages as these (extracted fairly randomly from Luke's Gospel only): 'you cannot serve both God and Money' (Lk. 16:13); 'Blessed are you who are poor, for yours is the kingdom of God. . . . Woe to you who are rich . . .' (Lk. 6:20, 24); 'Sell everything you have and give to the poor' (Lk. 18:22)? This selection, taken together with the previous evidence for the legitimacy of property, suffices to demonstrate (1) that the question of wealth and poverty cannot be reduced to one universal rule. Jesus' own approach was contextually determined. Though not evil in itself, material wealth can easily be counterproductive to the values or impact of the gospel. Where that is the case, its radical dis-posal in favour of the needy can become necessary. (2) It supports Johnson's conclusion that poverty as a gospel concept ought primarily to be understood as *theological poverty*[35] (that is, the psycho-logical or spiritual detachment from material values that faith

---

[32] Schmidt, *Hostility*.

[33] See Hengel, *Christianity*, 171–174, and for more detail Schmidt, *Hostility*, 103–162.

[34] Hengel, *Christianity*, 175.

[35] Johnson, *Sharing*, 80.

requires), albeit with quite possibly radical financial implications. 'Any of you who does not give up everything he has cannot be my disciple' (Lk. 14:33). Poverty is here the conceptual opposite of idolatry. The value of the synoptic evidence lies in the way readers are invited to learn from the struggles between such faith-poverty and material idolatry in the lives of individuals whose paths crossed that of Jesus. The force of the relevant texts is not that of a rule book, but that of a challenging witness – a witness that primarily aims to transform, not to instruct.

One's own use of possessions speaks either the transforming language of gospel proclamation or that of consumerist idolatry. Here we approach the theological heart of the matter. Followers of Christ are called to be challenging witnesses to others in the same way that the disciples and Zacchaeus and others were for us. Accumulation or disposal of wealth and commodities are not detachable from the kerygmatic quality of Christian existence. The answer to the question of the legitimacy of property and wealth resists opportunist privatisation. It would be equally simplistic, however, from a Christian perspective to equate *accumulation of property* per se with *consumerism*. This is so not only because the latter is by definition a modern phenomenon, but also because Jesus' own teaching on the matter suggests a greater degree of differentiation and contextual sensitivity. When he argues that it is more difficult for a rich person to participate in God's kingship than for a camel to squeeze through the eye of a needle (Mt. 19:24), he qualifies this in response to the disciples' expressed astonishment by conceding that with God anything is possible, including the possibility that many who are last will be first.[36] Obviously this is not envisaged as an automatic principle of universal reversal. Not everyone is able to accept God's generosity either to oneself or indeed to others, as the immediately following parable of the labourers in the vineyard illustrates. The parable's purpose is precisely to illustrate how divine mercy reaches out to those who are not offended by such

---

[36] Needless to say, this was hardly meant to encourage complacency, as the previous verses make clear: participation in God's kingship is precisely the reward for the disciples' willingness to leave everything behind (vv. 27–29).

generosity.[37] It is this paradigm of mercy that lies at the heart of Jesus' response to poverty.

Greed and Poverty in the New Testament World[38]

Above I referred to what Malina calls the 'limited goods society' in New Testament times. There are some major differences between that kind of society and (post) modernity. For instance, it was simply not possible to accumulate wealth and commodities as easily (relatively speaking) then as it is now. More fundamentally, though, it was not seen to be desirable to do so. Those who succeeded in increasing their wealth significantly were often regarded as dishonourable on at least two grounds. (1) Such social mobility often occurred at the expense of others. One might think of the landlord/tenant scenario or the tax collectors or traders who bought things in one place to sell them at a higher monopoly price elsewhere.[39] (2) It symbolised a disregard for social contentment, thus potentially destabilising society by displaying predatory behaviour or greed – the honourable thing to do was to remain faithful to one's social calling or background.[40]

In line with this mentality greed was regarded as negative not least because of its potential to cause social unrest. It had a clear communal dimension. Hence the advice to the rich young man not to defraud anyone and to sell his possessions in favour of the poor (Mk. 10:19–21).[41] As 1 Corinthians 6:7f. shows, such 'defrauding'

---

[37] Note the repeat of the 'first and last' motif (19:30) in chapter 20:16. Also, compare v. 15 with Lk. 15:28.

[38] Very readable treatments of property, poverty and social values in Roman society are found in Carcopino, *Life*, 61–75 and Daniel-Rops, *Time*, 138–158.

[39] Malina, *World*, 85.

[40] It might be suggested that this runs counter to the evidence of the parable of the talents in Luke 19:11ff. Cf. the incredulous response in v. 25: 'But Lord, he has already received ten talents'. However, this parable is not about accumulating wealth per se, but about Israel's leadership in the past and at the time of Jesus (who embodies the returning master).

[41] A similar dynamic is at work in, for example, Ephesians 4:28: 'steal no longer; instead use your hands to help the needy.'

could even be found in Christian circles, a particularly despicable situation. James 5:1ff. severely attacks the accumulation of wealth on the grounds that it is often achieved at the expense of those whose wages are held back because they were unable (or unwilling?) to enforce justice. It is far better to acquire spiritual wealth than to seek material gain, the latter being an attitude that 1 Timothy 3:6, 13 rules out as incompatible with being a deacon or indeed an elder, especially as such acquisitiveness is a significant threat to genuine piety and care for others (1 Tim. 6:5–10; cf. Tit. 1:7, 11[42]). Some passages urge the recipients not to seek material gain, but instead to practise hospitality (Tit. 1:8; Rom. 12:13) and to care for others (Jas. 2:15–17; cf. Mt. 25:34ff.).

What is today often regarded as social upward mobility and personal betterment would in antiquity have been observed with suspicion, not admiration. Day-labourers who 'made it to the top' would not only have been a rarity, but such 'success' would have been regarded as a betrayal of status. Equality was not a question of everyone being equally well off, but of honourably maintaining one's position within the social scheme of things, wherever that position happened to be. This is not to say that one had to tolerate one's lot, however badly one was doing economically. It would be a fallacy to interpret poverty in purely economic terms. Poverty denoted not in the first instance a lack of material wealth – although that clearly was part of the picture. Rather, it primarily denoted an existence on the fringe of society, perhaps because of ill health, having become widowed, being debt-ridden or imprisoned.[43] In practice, of course, social poverty and economic poverty converged only too frequently. The point to highlight, however, is that one was not poor simply by virtue of being a day labourer or peasant, that is, by belonging to a certain class, but by finding it impossible (for the variety of reasons mentioned) to live in line with one's inherited status. Where that social status *could* be maintained, whatever it was, there was no need for social mobility. It is in the light of this that James advises his readers or hearers to be content with what

---

[42] Cf. 1 Pet. 5:2; 2 Pet. 2:15; Jude 11, 16.
[43] Mt. 5:3ff.; 11:4f.; 25:34ff.; Mk. 12:42f.; Lk. 4:18; 6:20f.; 14:13, 21; 16:20–22; 21:2f.; Jas. 2:3–6; Rev. 3:17. For a more extensive list, see Malina, *World*, 85.

they have got rather than to be tempted by social or economic greed.

Given that in early Christian times social upward mobility was frowned upon by society in general and Christian ethics in particular, could it be argued that the latter represent a culturally conditioned peculiarity, rather than a foundational principle capable of reapplication in other contexts such as our own? I do not think so and would argue that, despite some significant differences, our Western European (and North American) societies at the turn of the millennium share enough aspects and practices of the New Testament environment to enable us to see biblical warnings against greed and the neglect of the poor as applicable to our own times. The similarities are that: (1) upward social mobility is essentially possible[44] (though it was by no means easy in early Christian times); (2) money is 'made to work', for instance, by means of interest charges;[45] (3) low social status and economic deprivation often converge, not least because of the fundamental tensions – both then and now! – between the doctrines of a market economy and the needs of the underprivileged. In sum, the fact that modern society applauds rather than frowns upon those who succeed in climbing

---

[44] Clearly upward social mobility presupposes some of the main tenets of a free-market economy such as the right to private property, the freedom of the individual to enter contractual arrangements, consumer freedom and the individual's free choice of a career. Equally clearly, these aspects reflect the economic liberalism of the nineteenth century rather than than the economic practices of the first century. Having said that, first-century Palestine did know incipient forms of these tenets (see Schröder, *Marktwirtschaft*). Centuries before the advent of Christianity, Aristotle (*Poltics*, chs. 8–13) discussed the differences between trading goods for the satisfaction of essential needs and the use of such goods for the purpose of financial gain, which can be maximised by imposing interest on borrowers.

[45] The practice of charging the consumer not just for the end product but for the initial investment in the machinery needed to turn raw materials into consumer goods is of course a post-industrialisation phenomenon. But the general principle of using interest as a money-spinner (thus turning money itself into an expensive commodity) is an ancient one: the buyer ends up paying not just for the goods purchased but also for the cost of money itself and for the dealer's profits and future investments.

the social ladder does little to challenge the basic validity of reapplying the New Testament warnings against greed in our own context.[46] Significantly, however, Jesus and the New Testament go beyond a mere critique of market- and consumption-driven ideologies by offering an alternative paradigm.

Jesus' Mercy Paradigm

One of the most difficult questions for Christians in a world of consumerism is how to address the question of poverty. What is poverty? It may be tempting to define poverty primarily in spiritual terms, thus avoiding the necessity to confront it at the material and social levels. One might attempt to appeal to Matthew 5:3 and 5:6 for scriptural support: 'blessed are the poor *in spirit*, for theirs is the kingdom of heaven' and 'blessed are those who hunger and thirst for *righteousness*, for they will be filled'. Some wish to adopt the opposite approach, counting on Luke's support when – in his parallels to Matthew 5:3 and 5:6 – he quotes Jesus as saying 'blessed are you who are *poor*, for yours is the kingdom of God, blessed are you who *hunger now*, for you will be satisfied' (Lk. 6:20–21). True, Luke's version does not have the qualifications 'in spirit' and 'righteousness'. Instead, one might argue, he appears to be more interested in what Jesus had to say about physical and social needs. However, he specifically points out that the disciples are the recipients of the beatitudes, thus compensating at least implicitly for the lack of reference to spiritual attitude. So who are Israel's 'poor'?

Sometimes, of course, the 'poor' are quite simply materially poor. For instance when Amos refers to the despicable practice of robbing the poor of their grain in order to build up one's own stores (Am. 5:11; cf. Jas. 5:4). Jesus' teaching actively makes provision for the materially poor by instructing the disciples to lend to those who cannot repay (Lk. 6:34f.), to 'sell your possessions and give to the poor' (Lk. 12:33) and to 'invite the poor, the crippled, the lame, and the blind' (Lk. 14:12). It is because they cannot repay

---

[46] A fascinating insight into the 'market economy' of first-century Palestine is given by Zoche, *Marktwirtschaft*, 49–61.

such generosity that the act of giving becomes a reflection of divine grace. Here we see not only the symbolic value but the transformative and restorative aspect of one's use of possessions. It is above all the letter of James that demonstrates that Jesus' approach of caring for (rather than defrauding) the economically powerless needs to be emulated by his followers.

The challenge for God's people to reflect his mercy onto the underprivileged is by no means new. It was never far from the surface in Jesus' disputes with the Pharisees and the religious leaders of Israel.[47] The difference today is that mass production, advertising and the acquisition of goods appeal to the consumer's increasing sense of having to satisfy one's own 'needs', thus banishing still further any thought in the consumer's mind of caring for the underprivileged. The whole notion of need has been tacitly moved to a different plane: what matters now is not so much what is actually needed, but how that which is *alleged* to be needed can be acquired *immediately*. This is in part the psychological rationale behind our modern 'interest-free credit' culture. How inconvenient it is, therefore, to be reminded by Jesus that to enter the kingdom one must be prepared not only to rid the self of 'this-worldliness' (Mk. 8:33–38; cf. Lk. 12:15), but also, as we saw, to give alms to the poor and to invite the underprivileged for meals as a reflection of God's kingship grace. The comparison between 'then' and 'now' demonstrates a clear shift in society's perception of 'need'. The needy ones are now primarily those who need instant interest-free credit to satisfy their consumerist cravings, not those who need to be provided with free grain because the last harvest was less successful than hoped for.[48]

---

[47] The first occasion where this issue raised its head was the calling of Levi. When the Pharisees and theologians expressed to Jesus' disciples their criticism of his table-fellowship with 'sinners' and tax collectors, he reminded them (by alluding to Ezek. 34) that he was only doing what the leaders of Israel omitted to do, that is, extending God's mercy into the lives of the needy. Instead 'the shepherds feed themselves' (Ezek. 34:2) and even criticise Jesus for making good their failure. On a different occasion Jesus tells the parables of the lost sheep (note again the allusion to Ezek. 34), the lost coin and the prodigal son to make the same point (cf. the parables' co-text in Lk. 15:1f.).

[48] For the experience of poverty in the Hellenistic cities of the Roman East, see Esler, *Community*, 175–179.

There is no suggestion here of a preferential option for the poor in the sense that Jesus' own invitations were restricted to such people. Even Luke, for whom 'discipleship and material possessions' is a topic of enormous importance, tells us of a number of occasions when Jesus enjoyed table-fellowship either with religious leaders and Pharisees or the 'sinners'[49] and those on the fringe of society.[50] The decisive difference is that many of the well-off who are invited to the (messianic) meal fail to turn up on the basis of less than credible excuses (Lk. 14:18–20). The idea of buying cattle unseen was as laughable then as it is now. Interestingly, in two of the three cases mentioned the suggested excuse revolves around the acquisition of material wealth. This is hardly a coincidence. We detect the same phenomenon elsewhere. When Jesus refers to Lot's wife as an example of how to 'lose one's life' (Lk. 17:32f.), we do well to remember that her failing was caused by her inability to 'let go' of the city that they had to leave behind (Gen. 19:12, 17, 26). The tragedy of that event as well as the one that Jesus has in mind according to Luke 17 – i.e. the destruction of another city, Jerusalem, in AD 70 – is that the warning had been given but ignored because of the inability to 'let go'. Genesis and Luke give expression to the sad irony that clinging to worldly values is incompatible with the receptiveness of heart that the acceptance of divine mercy presupposes.

It would be a serious mistake to apply these considerations purely to the sphere of personal salvation. The responsibility and accountability entailed in following Jesus are by no means restricted to the private and personal level. It would be one thing to opt for a material asceticism, but quite another to use one's possessions for the benefit of the needy. The fact that both Testaments include clear imperatives for the latter, rather than the former, suggests that the thrust of one's use, misuse or acquisition of material wealth ought not just to be confessional (of a 'witness' character), but restorative and 'materially' beneficial to others. It is highly doubtful that a consumerist worldview is compatible with this theological maxim.

---

[49] The term is in inverted commas because in the synoptic gospels it denotes a sociological category of people such as tax collectors, prostitutes and perpetually unrepentant Jews.

[50] A more detailed discussion of this is found in Moritz, 'Talk', 47–69.

The temptation is to place the task of restoration firmly in God's court. Though justified to an extent, we have to remember that discipleship means, among other things, participation in the establishment of God's kingship,[51] a notion that culminates in the setting free from futility and bondage of creation (Rom. 8:19–23). It is well worth reflecting, therefore, on what it might mean today to 'seek the peace and prosperity of the city' (Jer. 29:7) or to 'live as citizens worthily' (Phil. 1:27),[52] especially with reference to this all-pervasive phenomenon of consumerism. How can Christians hope to challenge society's obsession with consumerism by offering what is sometimes referred to as a counter-cultural lifestyle?

Theology and Praxis: Some Concluding Reflections

'The earth is the Lord's and everything in it, the world and all who live in it; for he has founded it upon the seas and established it upon the waters' (Ps. 24:1–2). We do not, strictly, possess anything. All things are the Lord's. This implies that 'things' are not evil in and of themselves, but that they can become so when treated as personal possessions or commodities for exclusively private use. When the wicked appears to prosper (Ps. 10), he does so at the expense of the poor and lowly (vv. 2, 9, 10; cf. Jas. 5:2–4). But the Lord is King (v. 16) and as such he will bring justice to the oppressed (v. 18). It is precisely this kind of divine kingship that the Christian is invited to share in. Sadly, modernity brought with it a redefinition of need in terms of the consumerist self, rather than the needy other. This effectively renders irrelevant the kinds of kingship aspirations embodied in Psalm 10. To recover this divine imperative means to reappraise our attitudes towards commodities on the confessional *as well as on the practical levels.*

If one had to capture this aspect of the theology of the New Testament in a slogan it would have to be along these lines: faith not commodities – mercy not greed. It is not that the New Testament

---

[51] Hence the promise to the disciples that they would participate in the judging of the twelve tribes of Israel (Mt. 19:28).

[52] This translation is suggested by Winter, *Welfare*, 103.

castigates the notions of personal property or consumer goods per se, but there is little doubt that these need to be subjected firmly to more overarching kingship values. Even if we allow for the cultural, social and economic differences between the age and environment of the New Testament and our own – as we surely have to – there still remains a firm imperative for Christians to question and subvert the worldviews and ideologies of this world. One of the dominant worldviews at the dawn of the new millennium is that of consumerism. It needs to be challenged, not because of its dominance, nor even primarily because of its subtle deception, but because it fails the test of some core values of the biblical storyline. Trust in God, the preservation and cultivation of this good creation and the rejection of all idolatry are just three such core values. Consumerism as the dominating *Zeitgeist* fails on all three counts. Our interest-free credit culture powerfully reveals the sinister side of consumerism: our society is effectively addicted to the point where we its members define our sense of value around the things and funds we control, even if this means living on borrowed money and exploiting the creation beyond sustainable levels. How can Christians hope to expose consumerism as the deceptive addiction that it really is?

Consider the following possibilities: (1) When purchasing luxury items, a believer could donate an additional unspecified percentage of their value towards the needs of those who really are needy. (2) Instead of buying new cars (which lose value the moment they are driven out of the showroom), Christians could decide to buy relatively new second-hand cars, giving the difference towards God's work among the needy in this world. It is doubtful whether either of these practices actually qualifies as 'sacrificial giving', but would they not send much needed signals in a deranged world of consumerist frenzy? It is left to the reader to imagine how significantly the cause of God's kingship could be furthered by the funds generated in this way. Quite apart from the monetary value to God's kingdom and the materially poor of such decisions, one would hope that they would result both in our own increased appreciation of the immense symbolic value of our financial transactions and in a much improved public perception of gospel values. If as God's children 'we are symbols of ourselves' and if 'everything in the earth is the Lord's', Christians ought to be more than willing to demonstrate these truths in the way they handle the assets God has entrusted to them.

Bibliography

Borg, M., *Conflict, Holiness and Politics in the Teaching of Jesus* (Harrisburg: Trinity, 1998)

Carcopino, J., *Daily Life in Ancient Rome* (Yale: Yale University Press, 1968)

Daniel-Rops, H., *Daily Life in the Time of Jesus* (Ann Arbor: Servant, 1980)

Dodd, C. H., *The Parables of the Kingdom* (London: Nisbet, 1961)

Esler, P., *Community and Gospel in Luke–Acts* (Cambridge: Cambridge University Press, 1980)

Glasson, F., *Jesus and the End of the World* (Edinburgh: Saint Andrew Press, 1980)

Hathaway, B., *Beyond Renewal: The Kingdom of God* (Milton Keynes: Word, 1990)

Hengel, M., *Earliest Christianity* (London: SCM, 1979)

Johnson, J., *Sharing Possessions* (London: SCM, 1981)

Lohfink, G., *Braucht Gott die Kirche?* (Freiburg: Herder, 1998)

Malina, B., *The New Testament World: Insights from Cultural Anthropology* (London: SCM, 1983)

Moritz, T., 'Dinner Talk and Ideology in Luke: The Role of the Sinners', *European Journal of Theology* 5:1 (1996), 47–69

Nickelsburg, G., 'Riches, the Rich and God's Judgement in 1 Enoch and Luke' *New Testament Studies* 25 (1978), 325–44

Schmidt, T., *Hostility to Wealth in the Synoptic Gospels* (Sheffield: Academic Press, 1987)

Schröder, H., *Die Evangelien und die soziale Marktwirtschaft im Jahre 0*, unpublished paper (Karlsruhe, 1980)

Winter, B., *Seek the Welfare of the City* (Grand Rapids: Eerdmans; Carlisle: Paternoster, 1994)

Wright, N. T., *Jesus and the Victory of God* (London: SPCK, 1996)

—, *The New Testament and the People of God* (London: SPCK, 1992)

York, J., *The Last Shall Be First: The Rhetoric of Reversal* (Sheffield: Academic Press, 1991)

Zoche, H., *Jesus und die Marktwirtschaft* (Frankfurt: Knecht, 1999)

5

Consuming God's Word: Biblical Interpretation and Consumerism

Craig Bartholomew

Where there is no prophecy, the people cast off restraint
Proverbs 29:18 (NRSV)

Introduction

Consumerism is an idol that Christians are in danger of being seduced by. It competes to become the story within which we live our lives. Now, of course, the Bible warns us very strongly against idols – we are to have no other God beside Yahweh! In practice, however, idols are not always easy to spot, especially when they make room for God and Christianity . . . but on *their* terms.

One of the characteristics of a mature ideology is, according to Bob Goudzwaard, that

the end distorts genuine norms and values. They are filled with a new content until they become useful instruments in motivating people to pursue the end. This distortion especially affects Christ's commands to walk in his truth, to do justice, and to love our neighbours as ourselves. The distortion of these norms betrays an ideology. For with them an ideology touches the human heart and reveals itself as false revelation.[1]

---

[1] Goudzwaard, *Idols*, 24f.

It is precisely this type of strategy that consumerism adopts in western culture. Pressure is not put on Christians to stop being Christians, but they are tempted to let their Christianity become another product in the market place.

In the battle against idolatry the Bible occupies a central place. It tells, as Gordon McConville and Thorsten Moritz's chapters make clear, a very different story to that of consumerism. Thus it is particularly disconcerting when the Bible itself is taken into the consumer camp and has the critical edge of its story removed by making it yet another consumer product that people use when they so desire and how they desire. In this chapter we will take note of tendencies in this direction in academic and church circles, and then suggest ways to 'consume' the Bible so that we are inoculated against the idols of our day.

Consuming the Bible in the Academy

For a long time now it has been a struggle to take the Bible seriously as God's word in university settings. At least, though, there was agreement that the Bible did have a meaning and the debate was over its true meaning. Now, however, the *postmodern* turn is being felt all over the academy and not least in biblical studies. Its effect in biblical studies has been to undermine the idea that the biblical texts have true meanings and to inaugurate a time of fragmentation and pluralism. Biblical scholars face a smorgasbord of alternative ways of reading the Bible and there is considerable resistance to attempts to argue for a *right* way to read the Bible.

In British Old Testament studies the scholar who has probably wrestled most seriously with the implications of the postmodern turn is David Clines of Sheffield University. And intriguingly the way forward that Clines proposes for biblical studies is that of a *consumer hermeneutic*! Clines rightly recognises that consumerism is a central element in contemporary culture and his proposals represent the conjunction of postmodernism, hermeneutics and consumerism.

Clines stresses the actual and, in his opinion, desirable, pluralism in OT studies nowadays. This pluralism is related to the contemporary recognition that all interpretation is contextual and cultural.

In response to our changed context, Clines proposes *a market philosophy of interpretation:*

> I want to propose a model for biblical interpretation that accepts the
> realities of our pluralist context. I call it by various names: a goal-
> oriented hermeneutic, an end-user theory of interpretation, a market
> philosophy of interpretation, or a discipline of 'comparative interpre-
> tation'. . . . First comes the recognition that texts do not have
> determinate meanings. . . . The second axis for my framework is
> provided by the idea of interpretative communities. . . . There is no
> objective standard by which we can know whether one interpretation
> or other is right; we can only tell whether it has been accepted. . . .
> There are no determinate meanings and there are no universally
> agreed upon legitimate interpretations. What are biblical scholars then
> to be doing with themselves? To whom shall they appeal for their
> authorisation, from where shall they gain approval for their activities,
> and above all, who will pay them? . . . If there are no 'right' interpreta-
> tions, and no validity in interpretation beyond the assent of various
> interest groups, biblical interpreters have to give up the goal of
> determinate and universally acceptable interpretations, and devote
> themselves to interpretations they can sell – in whatever mode is called
> for by the communities they choose to serve. I call this 'customised'
> interpretation.[2]

Such an end-user approach could entail recycling old interpretations that were thought to have been superseded by the progress
model of modernity. These discarded interpretations could be
revived in a post-critical form to stock afresh the shelves of the
interpretational supermarket. Clines goes on to say that he regards
the literary turn in OT studies as the most important trend since
the middle of this century. This trend focuses upon the text in its
final form as a literary artefact, upon the reader and her role in the
construction of meaning, and upon hermeneutics and the nature
of language and texts. Clines particularly commends feminist and
ideology criticism. Feminist criticism more than any other form

---

[2] Clines, 'Possibilities', 67–87, especially 78–80. For a more popular
exposition of this position, see Clines, *Bible*, 91–98.

relativises the authority of the Bible because it takes its starting point in an ideological position very different from that of the patriarchal biblical text. Reading from 'left to right' is Clines' slogan for reading the text against its grain and insisting on addressing one's own questions to the text.

The Academy and the Church . . . and the Bible

For all the helpful aspects of Clines' approach – for example, his recognition that we all bring our own presuppositions to our reading of the Bible – Clines' proposals for reading the Bible in the academy are closely akin to consumerism – there is no right way to read the Bible, and readers should read the Bible in ways they desire and in ways that will sell. There is, I think, a real tension and contradiction between Clines' market philosophy of interpretation and his commitment to feminist and materialist readings since the latter require determinate discernment of patriarchy and ideology. However, his proposal that we read the Bible as we desire is representative of a widespread trend in the academy to choose whatever starting point one desires in approaching the biblical text, and this trend is a manifestation of consumerism in biblical studies.

Clearly, for Christians with a high view of the Bible, such an approach is bad news! As Walter Brueggemann, who has also written extensively on postmodernism and biblical interpretation, rightly recognises, consumerism in terms of faith must be watched carefully. Brueggemann is repeatedly at pains to distance himself from consumerism in his proposals for a postmodern approach to biblical interpretation.[3] In his section on the development of an evangelical infrastructure that will shape interpretation he says that 'if this evangelical infrastructure is not carefully constructed, the Christian congregation will rely on the dominant infrastructure of consumerism, and will not even discern until very late (too late) that the infrastructure of consumerism contains little good news.'[4]

---

[3] See Brueggemann, *Texts*, 27, 29, 40, 57.
[4] Brueggemann, *Texts*, 27.

A market-oriented approach is potentially disastrous to academy *and* faith, for both are put at the mercy of the market. There is a legitimate economic aspect to education and research, but to allow this to determine the product is to move in a direction in biblical studies akin to Thatcherism gone wild.

From one angle it is not surprising that consumerism has invaded the academy. In the western world, universities have become ever more secular and they are therefore vulnerable to the latest winds of western culture. Orthodox Christians will rightly lament the effect of consumerism on the academy. However, as Nigel Scotland points out in his chapter, the church also shows signs of being vulnerable to consumerism. For example, there is a fine line between being relevant and losing integrity, and in order to have successful 'ministries' many churches too easily start packaging the gospel as a product for consumers. Take television. Clearly this is a powerful and pervasive medium in contemporary culture, and many Christians have rightly seen the need for Christians to be active in it. However, as Neil Postman points out, television is a very different medium to oral and written discourse,[5] and 'It is naive to suppose that something that has been expressed in one form can be expressed in another without significantly changing its meaning, texture or value.'[6] Consequently, uncritical appropriation of television as a medium for Christian proclamation may be successful as entertainment, but may in the process disembowel the gospel message. Since Postman wrote in 1985 the lure of consumerism has increased exponentially. David Wells argues persuasively that

> the cultural context in which we live favours those forms of spiritual-ity, Christian and otherwise, that are marching to the tune of 1990s culture, rather than those that are seeking to be faithful to the God of biblical revelation. What so many of these new spiritualities have in common is that they are offering benefits for the self and asking for little or no spiritual accountability. Designer religion of the 1990s allows itself to be tailored to each personality. It gives but never takes;

---

[5] See Miles, *Consumerism*, 77–79 and 140–142, for a discussion of the role of television in the information age.

[6] Postman, *Death*, 117.

it satisfies inner needs but never asks for repentance; it offers mystery and asks for no service. It provides a sense of Something Other in life but never requires that we stand before that Other.[7]

There is thus a real danger in the academy and in the church of the Bible and its message becoming just another product in the market place. How can we read the Bible so as to avoid this snare of consumerism?

'Consuming' the Bible

The Bible has much to say about idolatry. Redemption is all about being rescued from false gods 'to serve the living and true God'. The latter phrase comes from 1 Thessalonians 1:9. The whole of 1 Thessalonians 1 is relevant to our discussion because in it Paul specifically links the message of the gospel coming in power and the turning of the Thessalonians from idols to the true God. The effect of exposure to the gospel ought to be a turning away from idols. And if we use the expression in verse 8, 'the word of the Lord', as a description of the Bible,[8] then we are reminded that a major function of preaching, teaching and reading the Bible is to free people from the idols of our day, including consumerism, to serve the true God.

However, we have argued that in the academy and in the church, there is a danger of the Bible being fitted into a consumer framework rather than it being allowed to critique consumerism. In the light of this deteriorating situation it becomes urgent to ask: Is there a way in which we can read the Bible so as to inoculate ourselves against the idols of our times, and equip ourselves to live for God in the midst of our consumer-oriented culture? How do we read the Bible *prophetically* in our context?

---

[7] Wells, *Virtue*, 80.

[8] In the NIV this text is translated 'the Lord's message', but the NRSV translation as 'the word of the Lord' is a more literal rendering of the Greek, which refers to the word (*logos*) of the Lord (*kurios*).

There are many ways we could approach these vital questions. As a way into the discussion, we will use Ezekiel's call narrative. Ezekiel prophesied at that very difficult time for God's people when they were in exile from the Promised Land because of their persistent disobedience to and rebellion against God. Ezekiel 1, 2 and 3 tell of Ezekiel's call to be a prophet, and in 2:8–3:11 there is a fascinating account of God telling Ezekiel to eat, or consume, his word!

'But you, son of man, listen to what I say to you. Do not rebel like that rebellious house; open your mouth and eat what I give you.' Then I looked, and I saw a hand stretched out to me. In it was a scroll, which he unrolled before me. On both sides of it were written words of lament and mourning and woe. And he said to me, 'Son of man, eat what is before you, eat this scroll, then go and speak to the house of Israel.' So I opened my mouth, and he gave me the scroll to eat. Then he said to me, 'Son of man, eat this scroll I am giving you and fill your stomach with it.' So I ate it, and it tasted as sweet as honey in my mouth.

He then said to me: 'Son of man, Go now to the house of Israel and speak my words to them. . . .' He said to me, 'Son of man, listen carefully and take to heart all the words I speak to you. Go now to your countrymen in exile and speak to them.' Say to them, 'This is what the Sovereign LORD says', whether they listen or fail to listen.'

If there is a danger today of Christians consuming the Bible so that it becomes just another product in the market place, Ezekiel's call narrative suggests a completely different way of consuming the word. Prophets in Israel always faced the temptation to tell their hearers what they wanted to hear by tailoring their messages to the desires of the Israelites and so succumbing to the idols of the day. But the true prophet was called to convey God's word to his people whether they liked it or not. Time and again the prophets were called to stand with God against the lifestyle of the Israelites, often at great cost to themselves.[9] Ezekiel was no exception – he had to make quite clear to the Israelites why they were going into or were

---

[9] Cf. the struggles of Jeremiah in particular.

in exile, namely, because they had persistently rebelled against God. They and not God had broken the covenant!

That was no easy task, as God's call to Ezekiel makes clear. The description of Ezekiel as 'mortal',[10] or more precisely as 'son of man', highlights the vulnerable humanity of Ezekiel and thereby alerts us to the daunting nature of the task he is called to. Ezekiel must be the channel for relating the word of God to the life of the people of God as a whole, and that will not win him popularity. To help equip him for that task he is handed a scroll. Unusually, this scroll is full of writing on both the front and the back and this writing represents words of lamentation and mourning and woe!

In this highly creative picture the scroll represents the word of God that Ezekiel is to deliver to the Israelites.[11] The lamentations and words of mourning represent not the content of the message but its *effect* – Ezekiel's message is one of judgement and condemnation before it is one of hope. Standing in God's presence means that Ezekiel cannot just sympathise with the sufferings of God's people – he must bring a critical, covenantal perspective to bear so that they can understand the path back to God via repentance.

In order to engage in such a ministry, Ezekiel must be shaped by God's perspective at the deepest level of his being – this is what is involved in his consumption of the scroll. Far from this consuming of the word bringing the word into line with contemporary culture, this consumption will equip Ezekiel to bring Israel into line with God's perspective, a move that is at the heart of biblical prophecy. Especially in the first part of his ministry, Ezekiel is called to pronounce God's judgement on Israel. His vision of God alerts him to the difference between Yahweh's way and Israel's way. The word he receives from God provides him with a critical perspective on his contemporary culture. Surely it is just as true that the ministry of the gospel alerts us to the possible differences between God's way and our way, whether that be the way of our culture or often of the church. But how does it do this? How do we consume the Bible so as to be equipped to resist the idols of our day – particularly consumerism – and forge positive ways forward that honour God?

---

[10] So the NRSV.

[11] Cf. Ezek. 3:10: 'all my words'.

This story of Ezekiel's call helps us to answer these crucial questions in a variety of ways. It reminds us firstly that a prophetic ministry – a ministry that brings God's word to bear on his people and his world – is founded on *the authority of God's word*. It is solely on the basis of a word from God that Ezekiel is able to relate prophetically to Israel in their desperate situation.

In the post-New Testament context in which we may affirm the *prophethood* of all believers[12] it is worth reminding ourselves that without a strong doctrine of the authority of Scripture as God's infallible word, we have no adequate basis for a prophetic critique of our time and of our church. This century we have seen a wonderful recovery by evangelicals of a social conscience and a sense of the comprehensiveness of God's reign. In his very useful book *Transforming the World? The Social Impact of Evangelicalism* David Smith tracks evangelicalism's loss and recovery of a comprehensive vision. He rightly notes that evangelicalism's 'inability to unite the personal and the social aspects of religion, to see mission as embracing both the declaration of the word of God and the practice of the deeds that demonstrate the love and justice of God, remained one of evangelicalism's consistent, and most damaging, failures.'[13] It was particularly the Lausanne conference in 1974 that helped evangelicals recover a creation-wide sense of God's purposes. However, as evangelicals have increasingly woken up to the challenges and joys of cultural involvement, signs are emerging of a loss of confidence in basic Christian orthodoxy and in some cases a far too ready embrace of postmodernism.[14] If we fail to root

---

[12] By the prophethood of all believers I refer to the responsibility of all Christians to receive and relate God's word to all of life. See, for example, Acts 2:17. For a brief discussion of this point in relation to preaching, see Stephens, 'Preaching', 787–792. In Ezekiel 2:8–3:11 there is already a strong link between Ezekiel's reception of God's word and Israel's reception of it. 2:8 contrasts Israel's rebellion with Ezekiel's receptive eating of what God gives to him, implying that Israel too should receive God's word in this way.

[13] Smith, *Transforming*, 69.

[14] See, for example, the concerns expressed in Barclay, *Evangelicalism*. See my review of Barclay and other books on contemporary evangelicalism in Bartholomew, 'Evangelical', 9f., 34f.

ourselves in the word and succumb to the prevalent contemporary historicism, we will be reduced, as O'Donovan so ably argues, to being able only to 'speak for the culture against the culture, as the representative of a new strand in the culture that will fashion its future.'[15]

It is thus crucial that evangelicals maintain a high view of Scripture, but this is no easy task in our context. Amidst contemporary postmodernism, which privileges the reader as the locus of textual meaning and simultaneously denies determinate meaning for texts, it is a real challenge to hold on to any doctrine of the perspicuity of Scripture. But it is a challenge Christians must face up to, affirming that 'the Bible is the Word of God, record and tool of his redeeming work. It is the Word of Truth, fully reliable in leading us to know God and have life in Jesus Christ.'[16]

Ezekiel's call reminds us that a transcendent rootage in God is fundamental for a prophetic ministry, so that orthodoxy in the sense of a clear understanding of God as outside of creation and as having spoken in Christ is vital. But his call is simultaneously a clear call to a faith that transforms our lives and is not just a sterile series of propositions. Another way of expressing this is to say that to avoid idols we need to allow Christ to capture our hearts, the wellspring of our lives, afresh. Scripture has to become again the story we *indwell*. Ezekiel has to consume the scroll and we must inwardly digest God's word if it is to shape our lives.

In this respect the renewed interest in spirituality holds considerable hope. Joyce Huggett and many others continue to remind us that taking Scripture seriously means allowing it to lead us into a deep relationship with God and from there out into his world in his service – what are sometimes referred to as the journey in and the journey out. Real recovery of the authority of Scripture must involve recovery of the *lectio divina* – that devotional mulling over of Scripture in our persons so that it enters our very lifeblood.[17] George

---

[15] O'Donovan, *Resurrection*, 73.

[16] O'Donovan, 'Our World', 963.

[17] See, for example, Vest, *Heart*, and the works of Eugene Peterson and Joyce Huggett.

Steiner refers to this way of reading in a remarkable passage in his book *Real Presences*:

> To learn by heart is to afford the text or music an indwelling clarity and life-force. Ben Johnson's term, 'ingestion', is precisely right. What we know by heart becomes an agency in our consciousness, a 'pacemaker' in the growth and vital complication of our identity. . . . Accurate recollection and resort in remembrance not only deepen our grasp of the work: they generate a shaping reciprocity between ourselves and that which the heart knows. . . . What is committed to memory and susceptible of recall constitutes the ballast of the self. The pressures of political exaction, the detergent tide of social conformity, cannot tear it from us. In solitude, public or private, the poem remembered, the score played inside us, are the custodians and remembrances . . . of what is resistant, of what must be kept inviolate in our psyche.[18]

Few things are as important for the church today as for Christians to find ways to engage with Scripture so that it is ingested and becomes a powerful agency in their consciousness. This is the sort of thing Harry Blamires had in mind with his notion of a Christian mind. More recently this has come to be referred to as a Christian worldview.[19] We will say more about this below, but the point to note here is that a Christian mind or worldview must be rooted in an existential faith in Christ, and this soil must be continually nurtured by ingestion of the word. Scripture, like Ezekiel's scroll, must be so consumed that it becomes the agency in our consciousness, the pacemaker of our identity.

Spirituality is crucial, but it must avoid a reading of Scripture through the grid of the modern privatisation of religion. A central tenet of modernity is the privatisation of religion, which allows freedom of religion but restricts religion to the private lives of citizens and keeps it out of the great public areas of economics, education, politics and so on. This century, too much evangelical spirituality has been of this privatised sort, with spirituality and the implications of the word reduced to quiet times and evangelism and with virtually

---

[18] Steiner, *Presences*, 9f.
[19] See Bartholomew, 'Relevance', 41–48.

nothing to do with public life. Ezekiel's call narrative is by contrast a reminder that a prophetic ministry relates to life as a whole.

Prophecy in the Old Testament is based on a covenantal view of life that is rooted in creation. Underlying all Old Testament prophecy is covenant. At Sinai (see Ex. 19ff.) God established his people in a legal relationship with himself that the Old Testament calls a covenant.[20] In this covenant the stipulations governing the lifestyle of the people of God are set out in general in the ten commandments and in more detail in the other law collections. The ten commandments are thus utterly central to Israel's life as the people of God.

I think it is right to read the first commandment – 'You shall have no other gods before me' – as primarily referring to other gods in the cultus of Israel. There were to be no representations of any other gods in the temple or, more particularly, in the holy of holies 'before Yahweh'.[21] According to this reading, the first commandment relates primarily to Israel's 'worship' in the narrow cultic sense, comparable to Christians' worship in terms of their institutional church activities. However, from the commandments that follow it is crystal clear that what Christians do 'in church' has everything to do with what they do in the rest of their lives. The commandments following the first deal with work (third commandment), family life (fourth commandment), societal relationships (fifth, sixth, seventh), and legal testimony (ninth) and so on. This comprehensive range of covenant life becomes even clearer from the detailed laws that follow the ten commandments in Exodus and Deuteronomy, regulating all aspects of life, including health care, hygiene and environmental issues.

Covenantal law makes it clear that worship of Yahweh has implications for the whole of life, much as the concept of kingdom of God does in the New Testament.[22] The prophets continually recall the Israelites to loving obedience under God's reign and warn of the dangers of not returning to this. God's reign extends to all of

---

[20] See Dumbrell, *Covenant;* Bartholomew, 'Covenant', 11–33.

[21] See Phillips' insightful interpretation of the first commandment in his *Code.*

[22] See Dumbrell, *Covenant.* And most recently on this theme, Wright, *Jesus.*

his creation and God's people are to actively embrace this reign and embody it in their lives. Dumbrell in particular has shown convincingly how covenant in the Old Testament is rooted in creation, so that redemption is all about God's recovery of his purposes for his creation.[23]

This creation-wide, all-embracing perspective of prophetic ministry is absolutely crucial if we are to bring a critical perspective to bear upon our culture. Without such a perspective we will simply not see the urgent need to address issues like consumerism, and will find ourselves asking what this sort of issue has to do with the gospel! Such a comprehensive perspective is often sorely lacking in contemporary evangelicalism. Spykman speaks of the eclipse of creation in much contemporary evangelicalism,[24] and John Stott has stressed the need for a robust doctrine of creation in our theology.[25] If we are to operate prophetically in our culture, it is crucial we recover a biblical doctrine of creation and let this shape our worldview.

What does this all have to do with consumerism? Just this: that covenant regulates the whole of Israel's life; there are laws relating not just to cultic issues like sacrifice and tithing – the equivalent perhaps of our institutional church life – but also to environmental issues, health care, family life, politics and economics. In covenantal perspective, the whole of life is religion and thus the *prophetic* expectation is that God's character will shape the whole of the life of the people of God and not just the cultus. Covenant in the Old Testament and its New Testament correlate, kingdom, evoke the dynamic image of the whole of the life of the people of God under the winsome reign of God.

Amidst our complex modern societies God calls his people still to bring a kingdom perspective to bear on the totality of their lives and to resist the idols of the day. This implies urgently regaining a sense that Christianity relates to the whole of life or, in other words, recovering a biblical understanding of creation, and of redemption as re-creation.[26] Flowing out of this is the imperative for Christians

---

[23] See here also Wright's superb booklet, *Heavens*.

[24] Spykman, *Theology*, 176.

[25] Stott, *Issues*, 15–25.

[26] See in particular Wolters, *Creation*.

to recover and develop a Christian worldview so that they are equipped for thinking about our culture.

We should not expect the Bible to provide proof texts for answers to complex issues such as twentieth-century consumerism. What the Bible does do is outline the contours of a covenantal framework that provides the skeleton of a Christian mind or worldview. Wolters defines a worldview as 'the comprehensive framework of one's basic belief about things'[27] and argues, rightly in my view, that

> biblical faith in fact involves a worldview, at least implicitly and in principle. The central notion of creation (a *given* order of reality), fall (human mutiny at the root of all perversion of the given order) and redemption (unearned restoration of the order in Christ) are cosmic and transformational in their implications. Together with other basic elements . . . these central ideas . . . give believers the fundamental outline of a completely anti-pagan *Weltanschauung*, a worldview which provides the interpretive framework for history, society, culture, politics, and everything else that enters human experience.[28]

What we thus need is for Christians to consciously allow their worldviews to become more and more biblical, so that we can begin, as we have tried to do in this volume, to think through all aspects of our culture from a Christian perspective. Only thus will we exercise and embody a prophetic perspective in our own context and resist the idols of our day, such as consumerism. We cannot expect our preachers to be experts on cultural analysis and issues like consumerism, but we can expect them to keep us attentive to God and to sound forth from the pulpit the great vision of God's cosmic reign and the role of the people of God as his full-time servants. And those whom God has gifted as thinkers do need to engage in cultural analysis as part of their service to the people of God so that we know what time and place it is in our culture. The Reformed theologian David Wells has clearly seen this: 'part of the theological task must always be to ask what it means to have this Word in this world at this

---

[27] Ibid., 2.
[28] Wolters, 'Gutiérrez', 237.

time. *The only way to answer that question is to engage in careful, rigorous, and sustained analysis of the culture.'*[29]

The Bible as Ideological?

In this chapter I have pleaded for a way of consuming the Bible that will inoculate us against idols such as consumerism rather than allowing us to succumb to them, and I have suggested that the way to do this is to develop a Christian worldview that is integrally shaped by the Bible. One cannot assert this nowadays without being intensely aware that there is a strong strand of thought that argues that the Bible itself is a deeply ideological book with unhelpful nationalistic, patriarchal, ethnicist and sexist elements.[30]

Recently Terrence Fretheim has addressed these issues directly. He maintains that

> the [biblical] texts themselves fail us at times, perhaps even often. The patriarchal bias is pervasive, God is represented as an abuser and a killer of children, God is said to command the rape of women and the wholesale destruction of cities, including children and animals. To shrink from making such statements is dishonest. . . . To continue to exalt such texts as the sacrifice of Isaac (Gen. 22), and not to recognise that, amongst other things, it can be read as a case of divine child abuse, is to contribute to an atmosphere that in subtle but insidious ways justifies the abuse of children.[31]

Fretheim does not want to abandon the Bible as word of God but seeks to articulate a hermeneutic that takes account of these ideological elements with in it. He proposes a dialogical model whereby the believer and the believing community dialogue with the Bible to determine what is of God and what is not. Fretheim suggests four criteria for assessing biblical statements about God. Firstly, we can get help from nonbiblical sources like academic

---

[29] Wells, *Virtue*, 4 (italics mine).
[30] For a thorough introduction to socio-critical hermeneutics, see Thiselton, *Horizons*, 411–515.
[31] In Fretheim and Froehlich, *Bible*, 100.

disciplines and life experience generally. Psychology, for example, helps us to see how destructive Genesis 22 can be for children. Secondly, we can use other biblical material to assess texts we are concerned about. For example, Isaiah 49:14f., which portrays God as a loving mother, can be read against Genesis 22. Thirdly, the Christian community, as part of the people of God, has hermeneutic authority: 'From within this community, persons of faith have been given an authority to speak out against whatever in the Bible may be life-demeaning, oppressive, or promoting of inequality.'[32] Fourthly, Fretheim suggest six ways in which problematic texts may still be useful. For example, they may remind us that all language about God is inadequate or they may negatively alert us to issues that are really important, and so on.

It is not possible to deal here in any depth with the radical challenge that such socio-critical issues present to biblical authority. I raise them here because recovery of a biblical worldview in itself does not escape these challenges. Evangelical Christians face the considerable challenge of reading the Bible in its totality[33] and examining in detail how the Bible in its totality relates to feminism, power and issues of social location. In this volume we make a strong case for a biblical critique of consumerism, and similar work is being done and needs to be done on other contemporary issues. Personally I think it is unhelpful to concede as much as Fretheim does in terms of the Bible being itself highly ideological. To conclude, for example, that Genesis 22 is in danger of affirming child abuse lacks sophistication in the light of the powerful, nuanced readings available of this story in its canonical context.[34]

Conclusion

Consumerism as a way of life with religious overtones is an idol that competes for Christ's rightful role as Lord of all.[35] The Bible is God's

---

[32] Ibid., 108.

[33] An answer to these criticisms is to recover a strong notion of *Tota Scriptura*, the sense that Scripture is God's word in its totality and needs to be read as such on all these issues.

[34] See, for example, Childs, *Theology*, 325–336.

[35] See my introductory chapter in this volume.

major way of helping us to resist idols as we journey with God in history in his good creation. Thus there is much at stake in reading the Bible so as to hear God's liberating word. I have suggested, using Ezekiel's call narrative as a paradigm, that the way to resist consumerism as an ideology is to make the story of the Bible the framework within which we live and think, and then to bring that story to bear on consumerism. We must consume the word so that we are equipped to resist consumerism as an ideology.

We urgently need to recovery Scripture as God's word for the whole of our lives – not that Scripture supplies all the answers we need, for that would be to misunderstand the function of the Bible – in the sense that Scripture alerts us unequivocally to Christ as the clue to the whole of creation. It is as the church recovers this huge view of Jesus and pursues this clue in all areas of life that we will successfully resist consumerism and the other idols that compete with Christ's rightful claim upon our lives.

Bibliography

Barclay, O., *Evangelicalism in Britain 1935–1995* (Leicester: IVP, 1997)

Bartholomew, C., 'Covenant and Creation: Covenant Overload or Covenantal Deconstruction', *Calvin Theological Journal* 30.1 (1995), 11–33

—, 'The Relevance and Contours of a Christian Worldview', *The South African Baptist Journal of Theology* 6 (1997), 41–48

—, 'Being . . . An Evangelical', *Many to Many* 24 (1998), 9–35

Blamires, H., *The Christian Mind* (London: SPCK, 1963)

Brueggemann, W., *Texts Under Negotiation: The Bible and Postmodern Imagination* (London: SCM, 1993)

Childs, B. S., *Biblical Theology of the Old and New Testaments* (Minneapolis: Fortress, 1992)

Clines, D. J. A., *The Bible and the Modern World* (Sheffield: Academic Press, 1997)

—, 'Possibilities and Priorities of Biblical Interpretation in an International Perspective', *Biblical Interpretation* 1/1 (1993), 67–87

Dumbrell, W., *Covenant and Creation* (Exeter: Paternoster, 1984)

Fretheim, T. E. and K. Froehlich, *The Bible as Word of God In a Postmodern Age* (Minneapolis: Fortress, 1998)

Goudzwaard, B., *Idols of Our Time* (Downers Grove, Ill.: IVP, 1984)

Huggett, J., *Open to God* (Surrey: Eagle, 1997)

Miles, S., *Consumerism as a Way of Life* (London: Sage, 1998)

O'Donovan, O. T., *Resurrection and Moral Order: An Outline for Evangelical Ethics* (Leicester: Apollos, 1994)

—, 'Our World Belongs to God: A Contemporary Testimony' in *Psalter Hymnal* (Grand Rapids: CRC Publications, 1989)

Peterson, E. H., *Subversive Spirituality* (Grand Rapids: Eerdmans, 1997)

Phillips, A., *Ancient Israel's Criminal Code: A New Approach to the Decalogue* (Oxford: Basil Blackwell, 1970)

Postman, N., *Amusing Ourselves to Death: Public Discourse in the Age of Show Business* (London: Penguin, 1985)

Smith, D., *Transforming the World? The Social Impact of Evangelicalism* (Carlisle: Paternoster, 1998)

Steiner, G., *Real Presences* (London: Faber & Faber, 1989)

Stephens, R. P., 'Preaching' in R. Banks and R. P. Stephens (eds.), *The Complete Book of Everyday Christianity* (Downers Grove, Ill.: IVP, 1997), 787–792

Spykman, G., *Reformational Theology: A New Paradigm for Doing Theology* (Grand Rapids: Eerdmans, 1992)

Stott, J., *Issues Facing Christians Today* (Leicester: IVP, 1990)

Thiselton, A., *New Horizons in Hermeneutics: The Theory and Practice of Transforming Biblical Reading* (Grand Rapids: Zondervan, 1992)

Vest, N., *Knowing by Heart* (London: Darton, Longman & Todd, 1995)

Wells, D., *Losing Our Virtue: Why the Church Must Recover its Moral Vision* (Leicester: IVP, 1998)

Wolters, A., 'Gustavo Gutiérrez' in J. Klapwijk, S. Griffioen and G. Groenewoud (eds.), *Bringing into Captivity Every Thought: Capita Selecta in the History of Christian Evaluations of Non-Christian Philosophy* (Lanham: University Press of America, 1991)

—, *Creation Regained: Biblical Basics for a Reformational Worldview* (Carlisle: Paternoster, 1996)

Wright, N. T., *Jesus and the Victory of God* (London: SPCK, 1996)

—, *New Heavens, New Earth* (Cambridge: Grove, 1999)

Zimmerli, W., *Ezekiel*, vol. 1 (Philadelphia: Fortress, 1979)

6

Postmodernism Is Consumption
Alan Storkey

Consumption as the Faith

It is possible to think of consumption as an expression of individualism and self-worship. We could believe that the primary religious focus of modern life is the ego and see consumption as one of the ways in which the self gathers worshippers – my car, my house, my computer. Consumption can be seen as the means whereby the individual realises the wishes and ambitions of the self as end. For many years I accepted that view but, although it contains important insights, I think it has been overtaken. In the dynamics of our culture, consumption has now become the dominant faith and individualism, together with other subordinate commitments, serves it. Consumption is collectivist-individualist, nationalist-internationalist, the healer, the entertainer, the lover, the spiritual, the feeder and the consolation. It is the chief rival to God in our culture.

Even to state this seems odd, because it is so unlike God, or even the great principalities and powers of the past like the Roman Empire, communism or even capitalism. It is, after all, just shopping. How can the shopping trolley come to rival the Creator God? It is not through philosophy and apologetics. Nor even through persecution of Christians. Bibles and Christian books are happily sold. This is not really an ideology that can be taught as young people were taught dialectical materialism in the Komsomol. Indeed, the ideology often remains unexpressed, because when it is expressed, as we see later, it is banal – 'Drinking this brand of coffee gives you exciting relationships, whoever you are' is not intellectually persuasive. The faith lives and grows as myth because it has countless well-paid servants who, though often unhappy, go about their Master's business. The servants of the Lord God are dwarfed in number and working hours by the servants of consumption. Its ability to recruit seems unlimited.

Christianity, despite all the warnings in the gospels, has not even seen the challenge, the temptation, the lies, the enemy. We must consider sometime how completely the Christian community is unable to discern what is seeking to be the god of the age. I take no credit here. For about a dozen years from 1980 I was in the enemy camp studying his sacred texts, doing a dissertation on modern consumption theory. Consumption was in my head much of the time. But the focus of my study was a theoretical change in the discipline of economics, an important issue, but one which always kept me at one remove from the enemy. Now perhaps we can face it.

Our route is historical, because we need to see the building of a myth, a lie, a false religion, a faith. The focus will be on consumption theory. This is because it contains the 'theology' of the movement. Paraphrasing Keynes' words, shoppers are usually the slaves of some defunct consumption theorist.[1] History enables us to go straight to the intellectual heart of the faith, to see the structure of the mistakes and the cultural implications of the position. The theory unfolds with its own drama, as succeeding views signpost the inner dynamics of the religion. The journey has many turns and quickly invented dogmas, but in the end the enemy should be more fully exposed to the hurtful light.

The Significance of the Neoclassical Shift

We begin about a hundred and thirty years ago when three theorists, Stanley Jevons, Carl Menger and Léon Walras, initiated an overturning of economic theory which has come to be called the neoclassical revolution. There are many complexities to this change in thought, but a number are of deep cultural significance.

---

[1] Keynes, *Theory*, 383.

The first is the massive switch in paradigm from classical to neo-classical economic thought. The classical model thought in terms of cause and effect, from production to consumption. The neoclassical works from consumption to production. This was a change in the conception of economics. The classical outlook focused on how things are produced, with what combinations of land, labour and capital. The perspective had large and detailed weaknesses, and already human reliance on God and God's creation had dropped from the picture of the self-important landowners and manufacturers who generated this kind of economics. Its emphasis was on work, production, the division of labour and the use of resources. These were normally understood in communal terms – producing the wealth of nations or of groups – in the thinking of Smith, Ricardo, Malthus, Jones, John Stuart Mill and others. Life was work, except for the leisured few, and you produced what you needed. The neoclassical focus on consumption turned this conception on its head. Now consumers, through their choices and the operation of markets, called forth the chosen output from various economic agents. The switch was perhaps first enunciated by Whately. 'It is not . . . labour that makes things valuable, but their being valuable which makes things worth labouring for.'[2] On this view, the meaning of the whole economic system was to be seen in consumption. The economy was an efficient system for producing what people wanted. Both the classical and neoclassical models had serious flaws, but the latter provided a paradigm where the consumer were kings long before they actually were.

A second neoclassical theme was the end of the theory of value. Whately, writing in 1833, still thought in terms of value, but later economists believed that they could create a system that explained market price in terms of technical, mechanical or logical outcomes of consumer choices. After Jevons made the switch to this perspective in February 1860, value was neutralised.[3] This was actually a subtle and profound move, for it transformed economics into a self-subsistent logical system, cut off from the rest of life. The whole system rested on consumer utility and the costs of providing

---

[2] Whateley, *Lessons*, 33.
[3] Storkey, *Economics*, 54.

this. In this model, if you could justify something in consumption terms, it was justified or validated without reference to deeper life principles or issues of justice. To see the weight of this change, we need to reflect on the fact that money and prices are human creations, meant to reflect human values. To make them into some kind of self-referencing neutral system therefore misrepresents what they are. It also gives dominance to consumer utilities, which are the only non-technical input to the system. This model, pushed quite dogmatically as economic science, set up a consumption-driven meaning to economic life.

In reality, values should reflect God-given principles of life and fairness, and these in turn should be reflected in economic activity and prices. We should not bow down before what we create. This truth is inescapable and is the only valid way in which to see market and financial activity. But the myth says prices are self-determining, given consumer demand. It is this prototype that allows us to register the price of everything and the value of nothing, except what we buy. It is right, says this model, to produce anything you can sell. Of course, when first introduced, this perspective had very little weight compared to socialism and fascism. But in the 1950s and 1960s it came into its own and we are now seeing its fruit. Perhaps 20% to 50% of what we now produce has little or no real value to humanity. We'd often be better off without cigarettes, alcohol, fast food, weapons, drugs, media dross, technically fast but slow on the road cars, advertising, cosmetics, sugar drinks, security systems, lotteries, and many other things which sell. Rather than being goods, they are bads, indifferents or mere rubbish, and our degraded values merely make us poorer.

Utility Theory and the Ego

The great central tool of the neoclassical school was utility theory. This involved a number of other cultural conceptions. The first was its ego focus. In our egomaniacal age, we may not realise that this was a new idea in an age of collectivism and old style liberalism. The conception, drawing on James Mill and Bentham, was of a calculation in which the individual weighed pleasure or pain, relative cost and benefit to the ego. Initially, utility was conceived as a numerical calculus by Jevons (1871), but then it was reconstructed as an ordinal calculus of better or worse by Pareto (1906), Slutsky (1915) and Hicks (1942, 1956), yielding the pattern that students are taught as indifference curves at the beginning of their micro-economics courses. (Such curves are, in part, fallacious because the absolute amount of money you have does make a difference – ask the poor.) Already this approach moves beyond the merely individualistic. It focuses the whole economic order on the consuming ego and insists dogmatically that this is the only way of approaching the subject. Simply because it was possible to construct an ordinal logic of choice, this logic was passed off as neutral and even scientific to generations of students, when actually it was an expression of blatant egoism. This is conveyed in Veblen's famous words, penned in 1915:

> The hedonistic calculator of man is that of a lightning calculator of pleasures and pains, who oscillates like a homogeneous globule of desire of happiness under the impulse of stimuli that shift him about the area, but leave him intact. He has neither antecedent nor consequence. He is an isolated, definitive human datum in stable equilibrium except for the buffets of the impinging forces that displace him in one direction or another. Self-imposed in elemental space, he spins symmetrically about his own spiritual axis until the parallelogram of forces bears down upon him, whereupon he follows the line of the resultant. When the force is spent, he comes to rest, a self contained globule of desire as before.[4]

This view can operate at two levels, which are not unrelated: either as a philosophy of life by which people can live and act, or as an economic theory of consumption behaviour. We should note that on the whole, until recently, few people have lived this way. Principles, values, duty, regard for others, concern for the future, awareness of the weakness of hedonism, habit and many other priorities have made hedonism a minority culture and a partial one. You bought your mates a round, and did not just consume alcohol. Now, it is more dominant. Veblen's disdain suggests that this view does not offer a good theoretical description of human

---

[4] Veblen, *Place*, 73–4.

economic behaviour either. Its popularity within economics arose from the fact that it allowed mathematical determination of consumer decisions in principle. However, the calculations are actually too complex for a consumer or an economist (!) ever to make. This conception of the theory had great weaknesses, but it has come to have considerable weight because the marketing people have gradually learned to make it work. If colour, slogans, ego appeal, packaging and vehicles like sex, sun, water, excitement, happiness and reward can persuade the consumer to buy for pleasure, there is usually a higher mark-up and the consumer is led by the nose. Because the quest for pleasure goes on, because many consumers cannot admit to making buying mistakes, and because of behavioural addiction, the consumption patterns go on.

A second part of this theoretical framework was the supposed subjectivism of the consumer. This was particularly emphasised by Pareto, who wanted to preserve economics as the domain of logic and rationality, and relegated the consumer to the realm of inexplicable subjective preferences.[5] This perspective is wrong; it is easy to show that consumers operate on a number of logics, or preference systems, which make sense publicly and destroy the single logic of 'more and less' that Pareto tried to construct. This dualism cannot hold, but it is not the truth of this perspective, but its cultural power that concerns us at present.

At this point I wish to underline something which I repeatedly find gives historical insight. An academic formulation, even if it is not true, shows the cultural direction that will follow. This is because the formulation shows the weaknesses into which subsequent patterns of thought and behaviour will pour. Here a crude popularisation of this model moves onto the scene. There is the 'objective' business of prices, costs and products, and then there are subjective preferences that are handed over to advertisements to be channelled and shaped. Pareto forms a notion of the subjectivity and irrationality of consumers outside the logic of choice and, hey presto! nearly a century later that is how a lot of us are being treated. It is easy to ignore the invasion of the psyche that advertisements now constitute. More pushy than Goebbels, every fifteen minutes

---

[5] Pareto, *Economy*, 38–82.

for much of people's lives, and never subjected to critical scrutiny, they add up to near terminal indoctrination. Or haven't you noticed?

A further part of the theoretical structure was the 'principle' of the non-comparability of interpersonal utility. If you accept egocentricity as premise, then it is not possible to weigh what matters to one against what matters to the other in terms of utility. This argument is enshrined in what is know within the discipline as Arrow's impossibility theorems (1951). These theorems won him a Nobel prize, but they are entirely bogus. The premise is the conclusion. If we are egocentric utility maximisers, then it is not possible to consider issues of justice, fairness, wealth and poverty. But this is pure assertion. We are to love our neighbours. Unfairness and injustice are just that and they exist. Overcharging or selling shoddy goods may increase the shopkeeper's subjective happiness in a way I cannot measure against my own, but they remain a bum rap. Indeed, as Sen and others noticed, if you are concerned only with ordinal utility (the normal theoretical formulation in indifference theory), it is not possible to take into account the question of how much money you have or have not got, of riches and poverty. Sen (1979) got a Nobel prize partly for demolishing the argument which gained Arrow his. Arrow's position was no more than a technical elaboration of the attitude, 'I'm all right, Jack. Stuff you'. It claimed, although it did not have, some scientific status, as though I were more logical or scientific by ignoring my neighbour, my family, my friends, the world's poor and the shopkeeper when I made decisions to buy. But the culture arising from this attitude has drastic consequences. It rules out of consideration within the body of economic theory any question of justice, or relative wealth and poverty. It enshrines as the necessary way of seeing things a self-seeking subjectivity that can only consider questions of communal welfare as a non-economic postscript. This view was dismissed during the era when socialism held sway in Europe. Later, when the middle classes were looking for an ideology that would allow them to marginalise questions of justice and inequality in the era of Thatcher and Reagan, it flooded into the position of orthodoxy, even through it had been refuted at a range of levels.

We have thus seen that already at the beginning of the century there were paradigms that allowed a focus on the ego and an ignoring of my neighbour. They saw consumption as engaging with a subjective and even irrational motivation for choice and found ways to dismiss issues of justice and equality.

Modern Consumption and Maximisation of Utility

There is another assumption built into this view which deserves more extensive treatment. The whole of utility theory was based on an understanding of maximising utility. It is not possible to state this rigorously because it is not rigorous. It is merely the assertion that more is better, which, of course, often it is not. The assumption is of unlimited human wants in all significant areas of consumption. Actually, satiety is reached in most areas quite quickly. Two cars, three pints and one cigarette are all over my limit. Moreover, what we want is related to the way we live, what else we have and our concern for others. Some good later work has been done on limited wants and satisfaction equilibria. But, nevertheless, the idiom of unlimited wants has flourished. The lottery, a business which produces nothing and gets vast profits by moving money around inefficiently, has accustomed most of us to thinking of unlimited income and horizons of expenditure which exceed our wildest dreams. These wants may not be logical or reflect the way life is, but do reflect the fact that generating cultural attitudes can be extremely profitable. Advertisements, lotteries and marketing pressures can generate unlimited wants. Coveting can be institutionalised.

We are told that the generation of unlimited wants is good for us and is one of the bases of our affluence. This, of course, is tendentious. If we were not to overconsume in areas where we have been persuaded to buy more than is good for us, then more economic resources would be available to produce other things or cut down on our levels of work. Most governments have fallen in behind the idea that working for the highest levels of growth in gross domestic product is the only economic policy worth considering. So this theme of maximisation becomes a dogma, not because of its intellectual content, but because it is an ideology which the great corporations can run with. If we can be persuaded to think of consumption this way, then they have it made. We, meanwhile, are enslaved by the process.

This dogma finds expression on two levels. One is the personal level where the maximisation of consumption as dogma feeds into personal lifestyle. The result is a series of acute personal problems, which include the following:

- Overeating. The psychological pressures to overeat are enormous, as are the costs in terms of health. Many western health service problems could be solved if we ate properly. Something like seventy million Americans are on a diet, often spending more money to eat less. The economic waste of this process is incalculable.
- Overdrinking. Excessive alcohol consumption causes aggression, illness, poor work, broken families, road accidents on a vast scale. It damages the lives of millions.
- Domestic overconsumption. Many western people have too many things at home. Domestic storage space increases. The time required to maintain them and the cost of servicing them grows. Domestic units become less efficient. Relationships suffer, and there is a second round of inefficiency as families split up and multiple units are needed to service the same number of people.
- Time stress. Many people are working harder. Why this is the case we shall examine shortly. But the main time pressure which people face is leisure pressure. How will we fit in all those things which reward us? How can we maximise leisure consumption? The result is stress, even in leisure.

In a variety of ways people are being forced to re-evaluate this ego-centric maximising model because of its effects on their own lives, but, sadly, this often only happens after tragedy – family breakdown, ill-health, stress or chronic loneliness.

The consequences on the macroeconomic level are similar. If consumer maximisation is the assumed orthodoxy, then growth of the GDP is its macroeconomic equivalent. This has been the assumed central value in national policy for decades. Distribution of wealth and income is squeezed out of the agenda. So the GDP grows, but much of the growth merely reflects the inconsistency of consumption. We eat too much and buy indigestion tablets, use stimulants and sedatives when we need sleep, have an exotic, expensive week's holiday, when we'd be better off with two weeks' cheap holiday. We have security systems, insurance, health cover, therapy, fitness equipment and many other forms of expenditure which do not really add to our welfare, but just try to remedy failings in relationships and lifestyle. If we add together overconsumption and what could be called remedial consumption, we could be looking at a third of the GDP, an incredible level of effective inefficiency.

The New Teleology: The Austrians, Robbins and Ellul

There is another tradition in consumption theory that grows in a complex way out of Austrian economic theory. It has its roots in Aristotle and a much more teleological view of consumption. Here the focus is not on satisfaction and choice, but on purpose, on means and ends. The key theorists are Brentano, Menger, Böhm Bawerk, Meinong, von Mises, Hayek and especially Kaufmann and, through him, Robbins at the London School of Economics, and later Becker in Chicago. Here the human ends served by consumption go beyond economics, which is just concerned with the organisation of means to achieve those ends, as Robbins' famous statement put it. This is a much more dynamic conception. The organisation of means to the ends of consumption includes, in a fuller sense, production, work, purchasing and even goods themselves as instrumental to ends. There is a sense of time in the picture, and also a more realistic view of the way some goods function. We buy pans in order to cook, tickets in order to travel and washing-up liquid to do the dishes. Satisfaction does not dwell in any of these products. But as a total model for consumption, this understanding is no less tyrannical than the utility model.

Its fullest development occurs in the work of Gary Becker and other economists working in this means-ends maximising framework. As he says, 'I have come to the position that the economic approach [this approach] is a comprehensive one which is applicable to all human behavior.'[6] He and others then go on to look at the

---

[6] Becker, *Approach*, 8.

way marriage, polygamy, having children, a mistress and even being kind should be seen in terms of a future-oriented maximising calculus. Of course, sometimes life is like this. Children do sometimes make themselves unbearable until they are given sweets or a new bike. Wise parents recognise that relationships are better conducted on other terms.

We now have two models of consumption on the table, which correspond to two massive patterns of human behaviour: present-oriented consumption (POC) and future-oriented consumption (FOC). The first we have already encountered. It could be called hedonism or the search for maximum satisfaction now. This model drags the future into the present. What pleases me now is more important than what happens later. As a consequence, debt becomes a strong option. It gives me now what I pay for later. Because satisfaction is key, planning, purpose, development, and consequences pale into insignificance. Eat, drink, buy what you want with no concern for the consequences. Goods and services themselves become expendable and have no meaning beyond immediate consequences. Clearly, present-oriented consumption is with us on a large scale.

But so, too, is future-oriented consumption. On this view, work is the means to the consumption end. It is negative utility that will yield a later positive reward. Economic life is just a calculated effort towards these ultimate consumption ends, a massive process of throughput. And, of course, this is what many people feel. The strain of work, of production, is often negative, even unbearable, were it not for the consumption rewards which eventually emerge. But more than this, we are trained to push the ends, the consumption rewards, even more into the future – a bigger house, a better job which will mean higher rewards, a smoother car, more holidays, a cruise, a good pension, a nice burial. The pressure towards the future is so powerful that there is no room for the present – my friends, my growing children, the question of whether my work is good and valuable rather than just well paid. People are not able to live in the present, because the future with its ends and goals has so big a claim on them.

These two cultural types, POCs and FOCs, are encouraged and have great weight in the economy. FOCs lend to POCs. POCs borrow from FOCs. FOCs overwork in early life and often burn out. POCs have unstable economic lives. Advertisers appeal to each in different ways. FOCs want style, ultimate meaning for their purchases, but, of course, they will be disappointed. Like the rich fool, the self-serving ends will be inadequate, whether they face disillusionment or succumb to complacency. The costs of these views within our lives and the economy are vast. Life before God should be a more stable walk of faith, blessing, rest and good work.

We have to include within this section Ellul's Christian critique of this new instrumentalism. Means, or technique, have come to be dominant in the sense that we transfer faith from God and the value of humankind to the work of our own hands, the techniques that will save us and give us meaning. Whatever is technically possible is for the good, or will solve our problems. Drugs for health, missiles for peace, television for leisure, condoms for sex, paper investment for economic development. In Ellul's analysis, we lose our grasp on the ends and values that should order our technical development and become slaves to process and technique, allowing it to shape our values and become invested with magic. He wrote in 1960 and was he right! Consider the consumer industries of drugs, sex as technique, fast cars, the genetic manipulation of food, the arms trade and the glaring inconsistencies they have bred. Today, here in London, several million people will sit in cars which 'can do' a hundred miles an hour, crawling forward at 10–15 miles per hour, probably without asking why the technical promise of 'fast cars' is not realised. There is no wise structure of values and ends that shapes our use of technique; it becomes rampant and often destructive.

Friedman, Freedom and Consumer Captivity

Milton Friedman's economic reputation has fallen because his book on the consumption function is now discredited, but his popular impact during the Reagan/Thatcher era was substantial. His ideological focus was on 'The Free World', by which was meant the world where market activities were never wrong and supposedly consumers had the maximum choices. The credo 'Free to Choose' was seen as absolute, guaranteeing our way of life and containing its meaning. For economists who were awake, this position was somewhat odd given the existing studies of the problems of monopolies, imperfect competition, opportunity cost, retail monopsony power, brand loyalty and a range of other real-world issues which showed a lack of freedom in markets. But the consequences of this position were dramatic.

On the one hand, the dogma was choice; but on the other, the marketing aim was to capture the consumer in any way possible. Let us reflect for a while on this conflict between the ideology of freedom and choice and the commitment to consumer captivity and slavery. With some products, the captivity drive is overwhelming. Coca-Cola started out as an addictive cocaine product and since then has just been a brown liquid marketed through gimmicks to gullible behaviour addicts. Others seem a more straightforward choice, like buying tomatoes. But now, because we like tomatoes that are red, big, firm and last a long time, they are uniformly produced, or genetically modified, to look like this. We have a lavish choice of new cars, many almost identical, but almost none of small city runabouts, which would be cheap and economical, if less profitable to produce. The choices offered are often both bogus – twenty different brands of baked beans – and focused on what the marketing people decide we want. The consequence is extensive captivity. We are food junkies, fashion addicts, computer game epileptics, chocoholics, shoe fetishists, alcoholics, TV addicts, drug dependents, sports-gear obsessives. Companies win multinational wars bringing consumers into captivity. This has only been done with heavy manipulative intent over the last twenty years, and adults have readily succumbed. Children, who have been exposed nearly from birth, will be a pushover.

What is now becoming cultural orthodoxy is that we have freedom only to buy. Watch football, wear clothes, go for a walk, surf the Internet, date a girl and we learn it is a buying experience. Watch football and buy a shirt. Why? I have a shirt. Wear this and get your man. Do I want a man so gullible and stupid? These are not arguments. The appeal is to false images, herd instincts, the insecurities of children and adults. The weakness of the arguments is overcome by repetition. Visual mantras pull the fools in. Along with the 'freedom' only to buy is the prohibition against other things – thinking (for captive consumers need to be dumbed down), education, faith, relationships, art and family. We need more money for chocolate and less for health care. Consumption is now laying down its terms for the whole of life. 'Excessive' you say, burying your head in the catalogue.

Programming the Consumer and Advertising

Advertising is the fastest growing form of communication in the world. The average American (itself deep adspeak) watches eighty or so advertisements a day on TV as well as being exposed to hoardings and magazine, newspaper and Web advertising. This level of penetration into the daily lives of all of us is unprecedented by any ideological group in history. Of course, part of the package is the assertion that advertising is not ideological. . . . For almost all western people no religious exposure, no political conviction, no educational engagement comes within a tenth of the penetration of consumer advertising into their lives. It is privileged access, because advertisers pay and ads bring sales, and sales bring profits.

What follows has a particular structure, at one level pathetic, but at another level the most successful and comprehensive ideological putsch of all time. It is backed by the institutionalisation of lying. 'Thousands of customers are coming back to BT each week.' But thousands are also leaving, and we hear less about them. The consumer must be persuaded to buy. Even to state this premise is unnecessary for millions of workers in this field. But the method of selling is not to present the characteristics of the product, so that a measured choice can be made. (Even to talk of such an approach that emphasises truthfulness sounds off the planet.) Rather, some aspect of faith, meaning or personhood is appropriated to the product or service. Consumption becomes religious, but with a built-in eclecticism. It is epitomised by the T-shirt seller on Oxford Street who on the same stall sells shirts bearing the motif, 'Life is football', 'Life is a beach', or any other 'Life is . . .' which will sell. The question 'Is this inconsistent?' is nonsense within this worldview. What will sell becomes the truth.

But this is not truth as we have hitherto known it, but a process whereby products are linked to the inscape of persons. Let us list a few of the inner appeals which are made, premised on buying certain goods: confidence, innocence, relaxation, love, security, power, naturalness, fun, status, comfort, peace, happy families, romantic love, friendship, excitement, freedom from stress, sex appeal, personal attraction, health, youth, happiness, serenity and many more aspects of a good life are tied to products and services. Miller's analysis of 'Making Love in the Supermarkets' hits the mark, for this is where postmodern love is fabricated.[7] Like Gulliver, the postmodern person is tied down into consumption by a thousand fine threads and is asleep. The appeals of consumerism are pathetic in that they are not true. Consumer goods and services cannot give the qualities they claim, and can often not even contribute to them. Often the contradiction is direct. Cosmetics claiming to give a natural appearance instead cover it up. A person's attractiveness is obscured by impersonal consumer aids to being personally attractive. So we have an invasion which landscapes the mind, emotions and inner character of millions of people, even though it is fabricated of lies. This could be the most serious challenge to humankind of all time. The ability to swallow lies is one of the best indices of our ability to mess up, and we are now gulping.

The religion of consumerism only flourishes because the priests are well paid and because the lies are not called: 'Do you want a recession, or something?' But it demolishes other areas of life or bends them to its service. Politics becomes consumption of the Clinton/Lewinsky saga or other mindless personal dramas. Religion and our life in relation to God are drowned in the sea of shopping. Do not go to church, but come to a supermarket. Morality and the good life sink beneath the life of goods. Surprisingly, education, the commitment to wisdom, understanding, values, and learning are also easily defeated. Television as consumption outweighs the processes of learning in a child's life. Consumption has such a strong hold over culture that it is culture. 'That painting's worth half a million.' 'The classics? Do they sell?' The inroads of the arms trade, drugs companies and many other ardent consumer enterprises into the structure of higher education are breathtaking. So there are, it seems, no independent areas left standing before the onslaught of this ideology of salvation by buying. Marcuse's one-dimensional man and one-dimensional living have arrived. But the consumption myth is not even remotely true . . .

---

[7] Miller, *Theory*, 15–72.

Postmodernism as Consumption

There are many theories of postmodernism, and as a practising sociologist I have read most of them. I have several more of my own, including one that took something like ten years to develop. But much of the erudite and even arcane discussion of postmodernism misses the most powerful theory of all. Postmodernism is consumption. The deconstruction and fragmentation which is often identified with changes in approaches to text and philosophy is actually buying, advertisements, TV culture, in-your-face entertainment, shopping, pressure, thing-filled living — in a word, consumption. This is where the fragmentation is located and initiated, and much of the culture merely reflects these pressures. Further, culture is in principle fragmented because consumerism will use any cultural idiom available to generate sales. Advertising people are not scrupulous about their sources. If Bach will sell insurance, then Bach it will be as background, even though Bach relied more on God than insurance. Get it, whatever it is. Use it. Be effective. The next generation will think that Bach was sponsored by. . . . Conversion to buying supersedes religious conversion and is disintegrative. The psalmist's 'Unite my heart to fear thy Name' becomes 'Scatter my identity by buying'.

This is where academic postmodern theory does not see and understand the challenge. To reconstruct this revolution in terms of thought, even the type of thought which appears in academic journals, is to ignore the culturally dominant fact that a slick, vacuous advertising copywriter is trying to think up some slogan, any advertisement, that will sell. This activity has no intellectual content that is not parasitic and merely seeking a point of appeal. It is a principal dumbing down. It is required mindlessness. That is the postmodern challenge, the buying tide that actually persuades young people that McDonald's has some significance for life.

Gain the World and Lose the World

Of course, Jesus is there already. He spoke of gaining the world, and now the whole world is on offer. There is nothing, nowhere you cannot buy, it seems. But the very word 'consumption' gives the lie to this. The model of the world's resources being poured into the consumer, as if the whole world comes to us and we gain it, is precisely the lie. And there are other lies too:

1. Life is consumption, and consumerism can incorporate the meanings of life.
2. Consumption defines the dominant relationship we have with the world, rather than stewardship and care.
3. Life with God, others, creation, and ourselves can be ignored as long as the consumption relationship works.
4. The consumption model defines our relationship with things.

Jesus identifies the fallacy. Who we are before God and one another is prior: 'What good will it be for a man if he gains the whole world, yet forfeits his soul? Or what can a man give in exchange for his soul?' (Mt. 16:26). So Jesus relativises consumption in global terms. His prime focus is on the lie about the self that lies at the heart of this idiom. The gain is the loss. The gain to self is the loss of self. And the loss of the selfish self, given over to Jesus, is the gain of the true self. The consumption lie denies the self, community, the meaning of creation, God and even the proper character of the blessing of goods and services. Were it not for consumerism, we would be better off in terms of the quality of goods, services and life itself. This is not an anti-economic message, but the one needed to restore economic life. The cultural lie, pushed by a well-paid priesthood, is fragmenting the lives of millions and producing shoddy goods. Seeking first God's right ways is necessary for balanced economic lives.

We will be surprised when the fragmenter idol of consumption itself fragments. Recession, the fall of the dollar, the atrophying of compulsive buying and competitive world consumption will take their toll. But the test is whether by faith in Jesus and recognition of the truth, the west can move peacefully through this idolatry. 'And you who have no money, come buy and eat! . . . Why spend money on what is not bread, and your labour on what does not satisfy? . . . Hear me, that your soul may live . . .' (Is. 55:1–3). At present there seem to be many queuing in very smart cars on the wide roads that lead to destruction.

Bibliography

Arrow, K., *Social Choice and Individual Values* (New York: Wiley, 1951)

Becker, G., *The Economic Approach to Human Behaviour* (Chicago: University of Chicago Press, 1976)

—, *A Treatise on the Family* (Boston: Harvard University Press, 1981)

Ellul, J., *The Technological Society* (New York: Vintage, 1964)

Friedman, M. and R. Friedman, *Free to Choose* (New York: Harcourt, Brace & Jovanovitch, 1980)

Hicks, J., *A Revision of Demand Theory* (Oxford: Clarendon, 1956)

—, *Value and Capital* (Oxford: Oxford University Press, 1942)

Howey, R., *The Rise of the Marginal Utility School* (New York: Columbia University Press, 1989)

Jevons, S., *The Theory of Political Economy* (London: Macmillan 1924)

Keynes, J. M., *The General Theory of Employment, Interest and Money* (London: Macmillan, 1961)

Marcuse, H., *One Dimensional Man* (New York: Sphere, 1972)

Miller, D., *A Theory of Shopping* (Polity: Cambridge, 1998)

Pareto, V., *Manual of Political Economy* (London: Macmillan, 1971)

Robbins, L., *An Essay on the Nature and Significance of Economic Science* (London: Macmillan, 1984)

Sen, A., *Choice, Welfare and Measurement* (Oxford: Basil Blackwell, 1982)

—, 'Personal Utilities and Public Judgements', *Economic Journal* 89 (1979), 463–89

Slutsky, E., 'On the Theory of the Budget of the Consumer' in G. Stigler and K. Boulding (eds.), *Readings in Price Theory* (Illinois: Irwin, 1962)

Storkey, A., *Transforming Economics* (London: SPCK, 1986)

—, *Foundational Epistemologies in Consumption Theory* (Amsterdam: Free University Press, 1993)

Tiemstra, J., *Reforming Economics* (Lewiston: Edwin Mellon, 1990)

Veblen, T., *The Place of Science in Modern Civilisation and Other Essays* (New York: Caprice Books, 1969 [1915])

Whately, R., *Easy Lessons on Money Matters for the Use of Young People* (London, 1833)

7

Life and Death and the Consumerist Ethic
Gordon Wenham

The relationship of consumerism to traditional Christian ethics is often mentioned but rarely analysed. It is of course a vast topic that requires much more than an essay to do justice to. However, since this is where the differences between modern and traditional values are seen at their most contentious and those who resist consumerist values are often viewed as eccentric, we believe it is necessary to address the issues.

The most obvious recent collision between consumerism and the biblical way of life is Sunday trading. The introduction of the sabbath on which all ordinary work was banned and trading forbidden is one of the most striking and original innovations of the Old Testament. Other ancient cultures, as far as we know, did not have the idea of a rest day once a week; time for them was marked by new moons, days of ill omen, or religious festivals that occurred erratically. The Old Testament, of course, did have its annual festivals, such as Passover, Pentecost, Tabernacles and the Day of Atonement. But the weekly sabbath was more important than these festivals. Genesis 2:1–3 traces its origin back to creation, implying its universal relevance, and it is the only festival to be regularly called holy.[1]

So important is the sabbath in the Old Testament that it is included in the ten commandments given at Sinai, before even the prohibitions on murder, adultery and theft. But the Old Testament

---

[1] For a convenient summary, see de Vaux, *Israel*, 475–83. More fully Andreasen, *Sabbath*.

does not regard the sabbath as instituted at Sinai, it traces it right back to creation. God's working for six days and resting on the seventh is clearly presented as the pattern for human behaviour; for man, made in God's image, is supposed to imitate him. Very unusually, the sabbath is blessed: usually only living things are blessed in the Bible. God's blessing in the Bible leads to good health, long life, wealth, many children and God's presence, many of the goals of our consumer society. But whereas consumerism tells us these are to be achieved by unbridled desire and exchange of goods, the Bible implies they are granted only to those who take a break from their labours and devote one day a week to God. Indeed, Hebrews 4:9 regards the sabbath as a foretaste of heaven.

This pattern of activity was taken over by the Christian church in the time of Constantine, who made the day of rest Sunday instead of Saturday to commemorate the resurrection. But the principle of six days of work, followed by a day of rest, was retained.[2] Quite how strictly the day should be observed has been a matter of debate down the centuries, but the principle of a day of rest was accepted throughout Christendom till recently. But in the last decade laws have changed in the USA and the UK allowing Sunday to be a shopping day like any other, so that now Saturday and Sunday are often the busiest days of the week for shops. These consequences of Sunday trading were predicted by the Keep Sunday Special Campaign. The justification for this change was consumer freedom. If consumers wanted to shop on Sunday, they should be allowed to. If shopkeepers wanted to offer shopping facilities, they should be allowed to. It all sounds very civilised and reasonable, a step forward to a more rational flexible society.

But who are the main beneficiaries of these new trading patterns? Clearly though shops are open longer, people are not going to buy any more; they just spread their purchases over a longer period. This leads to increased costs, at least for those shops that do not increase their market share, and ultimately to higher average prices for the consumer. Because shop assistants and managers have to work on Sundays, they will have less time with their families at the weekend,

---

[2] For a discussion of the earliest Christian practice, see Beckwith and Stott, *Day.*

so family life will be weakened. Worst affected are the small shop-keepers, who now have to open seven days a week if they are not to lose the valuable weekend trade to the supermarkets and depart-ment stores. Our local DIY man has only taken three days off in the last year. Sunday trading is yet another device of the supermarket chains to squeeze the small shopkeeper. And when the small local shops are forced out of business, everyone will have to travel to out-of-town trading estates or downtown shopping malls to buy everything, with all the extra traffic that will generate, let alone the cost of transport.[3] Already British roads are nearly as busy on Sun-days as on other days of the week, and the town centres noisy. A visit to Germany and France is a reminder of what the British Sunday used to be like.

This example illustrates many aspects of consumerist ethics. It is driven by the goal of making money, especially by large businesses. What seems on the surface to be promoting individual freedom and convenience leads to the oppression of the weak, in this case the small shopkeepers and those who do not own cars and cannot go to the superstores. Furthermore, society as a whole suffers through the weakening of family bonds and the noise and pollution generated for seven instead of six days a week. Finally, what seems a modern inno-vation represents rather a reversion to a pattern of life in pre-biblical times, when erratic national or religious holidays were the only times the whole community rested and celebrated together.

Definition of Consumerist Ethics

Discussions of consumerism and ethics tend to focus on the clash between God and mammon, on how advertising teaches us to covet, to be discontented with our lot, buy more than we should, give too little away, and waste the world's resources.[4] All this is fair

---

[3] For the adverse effects of out-of-town superstores on small city-centre shops, see Miles, *Consumerism*, 57–9.

[4] 'At base, consumerism derives its power from a systematic and flagrant denial of the commandment prohibiting covetousness. Its consequences are thus predictably and universally bad. Following Christ entails a sharp break with consumerism' (Lyon, 'Consumerism', 257).

comment and most Christians are vaguely uncomfortable about their unwitting conformity to the standards of our consumerist world instead of the renewal of their mind according to the will of God. Other essays in this volume have explored the biblical teaching on wealth, so I do not propose to go over this ground again. Rather, I shall try to show how the consumerist ethic is affecting areas of activity that superficially have very little to do with wealth and how we use it.

Having illustrated the clash between traditional Christian ethics and consumerism over Sunday, I now want to explore the different approaches to birth, marriage and death in the two traditions before offering some observations about some of the weaknesses and self-contradictions of consumerism. But before looking at these contemporary debates, we need to define more clearly the nature of consumerism and look at its historic roots.

Slater offers the following definition of consumerism. Consumer culture is an 'arrangement in which the relation between lived culture and social resources . . . is mediated through markets.'[5] 'Consumer culture is about continuous self-creation through the accessibility of things which are themselves presented as new, modish, faddish or fashionable, always improved and improving.'[6] 'Furthermore, since people in consumer cultures are free to buy and sell what they like,' Slater argues that consumerism is at heart amoral if not immoral. 'If there is no principle restricting who can consume what, there is also no principled constraint on what can be consumed: all social relations, activities and objects can in principle be exchanged as commodities. This is one of the most profound secularisations enacted by the modern world.'[7]

Now although consumerism only became a fashionable and politically respectable philosophy under Reagan and Thatcher in the 1980s, its origins are much earlier. It developed strongly in the post-war years as manufacturing capacity exceeded demand and people's desires had to be stimulated by advertising. But in incipient form it was already present in the Victorian era in the wake of the

---

[5] Slater, *Culture*, 8.
[6] Ibid., 10.
[7] Ibid., 27.

industrial revolution. Its essential philosophy may be traced back to the enlightenment, with its denial of moral absolutes and the assertion of individual human autonomy by such writers as Descartes, Hume and Rousseau.[8]

Clapp identifies two central commitments that characterise contemporary consumerism.

> The first is the commitment to self-creation and autonomous self-definition. We are told today that we are, or at least ought to be, entirely free to make whatever we would of ourselves; and so long as our projects of self-construction do not obviously interfere with anyone else's, we must not be hindered by tradition, custom, law or outmoded notions of 'human nature' as we fashion our own identities This commitment amounts finally to a repudiation of the belief in moral order. The second commitment entails shrinking the range of possible human aspirations to those circumscribed by secular existence. We may construct ourselves entirely as we see fit, so we are also told today, as long as we remain within the confines of this world and within the limits of the here and now.[9]

Birth, Marriage and Death

The consumerist ethic is profoundly affecting the modern approach to the fundamental points of human life, namely birth, marriage and death. Traditionally these have been seen as fixed points in human existence that had to be accepted and that entailed certain unalterable obligations by those involved and by society as a whole. Thus marriage was regarded as the normal lifestyle of most adults, carrying with it the obligations of lifelong fidelity – 'for better for worse, for richer for poorer, in sickness and in health . . . till death us do part' – and bringing up children.[10]

---

[8] For a review of the history of consumerism, see ibid., 10–83.

[9] Clapp, *Passion*, 20.

[10] The procreation of children is defined in the Anglican prayer book as the first purpose of marriage, echoing the first command given to the human race in Genesis 1:28 'Be fruitful and multiply', cf. Ps. 127; 128.

The consumer marries because marriage will serve his or her interests as he or she understands them at the moment. Commitment in the Christian way of life is an ideal and a goal; commitment in the consumer way of life is an instrumental and typically temporary good. Like any careful contract, marriage in the consumer ethos should continually be open to re-evaluation. If at any point it fails to promote the self-actualisation of one spouse or the other, the option of ending the partnership must be available. In the Christian way of life, lifetime monogamy makes sense. In the consumer way of life, serial polygamy (a succession of mates over a lifetime) is a much more sensible practice. A high increase in divorce rates signals many things, but one of them surely is that consumption is our way of life.[11]

Whereas traditional Christians, as well as Jews and Moslems, regarded procreation and child-rearing as intrinsic to marriage, modern consumerism regards this as quite optional. 'Use contraception until you feel like having a child' is the modern philosophy. 'Do not let children ruin your career, and certainly avoid having too many because that will spoil your standard of living and tie you down. You will not be able to enjoy yourself.' Such is the advice proffered by consumerist parents and agony aunts to newly-weds.

Frankly, consumption as a way of life renders it difficult to justify having children, since children represent the commitment of a lifetime. In the wonderfully apt phrase of novelist Michael Dorris, children 'hold us hostage to the future.' They limit a parent's mobility, dictate through their needs the spending of much parental money and create 'agendas' a parent otherwise would never have imagined, let alone chosen.[12]

Running through the consumerist ethic is the idea of individual choice or human autonomy. Thus if naturally fertile couples may choose not to have children, it is equally permissible for infertile couples, heterosexual or homosexual, and single women or post-menopausal women to seek to have children by whatever

---

[11] Clapp, *Passion*, 193.
[12] Ibid., 194.

means modern medical technology can devise. Here the driving force is essentially the desires of the would-be parent, who cannot accept his or her childlessness. The production of a child is to satisfy this longing. The long-term welfare of the child seems to figure little in the weighing of the benefits of these expensive procedures. How will a woman in her seventies cope with the needs of an energetic adolescent? How will a child learn to be a good spouse if he or she does not have the example of both a father and mother relating to each other? What will the child think if she discovers her parents brought her into being through *in vitro* fertilisation (IVF), egg donation or surrogate motherhood? Who are her real parents? What will a boy think when he realises he has been cloned from his father or brother? And what about all the 'spare' embryos that go to waste in these procedures? Waste is endemic in consumer cultures, but how many human lives may be discarded to make one child?[13]

These are some of the issues raised by this attempt to make babies on demand to satisfy the wishes of would-be 'parents'. Oliver O'Donovan has drawn attention to the way in which modern techniques distort the whole concept of the child and parenthood. Essentially we are manufacturing children instead of procreating them, making them instead of begetting them. We beget children who are of the same nature as ourselves, we make things which are different in nature from us. These artificial techniques for circumventing childlessness, O'Donovan argues, change the whole child-parent relationship and sever the link between the relational and procreational aspect of sexual relationship. Normally a child's conception is the fruit of an act of love between its parents, but with IVF there is no necessary linkage between an act of sexual intercourse between the couple and the conception of the child. The baby is made in the doctor's laboratory and then implanted into a

---

[13] In 3 years (1991–94) 302,156 embryos were produced by IVF in Britain. This led to 7,011 live births. Thus only 2.3% of all embryos generated survived as born children. Some 90,000 spares were thrown away immediately. About 100,000 were transferred to wombs, but 93% died before coming to birth. Of the remaining embryos 27,524 were used in research, and 64,161 were frozen (*Life News*, 9). (*Life News* is published by LIFE–Save the Unborn Child, Life House, 1A Newbold Terrace, Lemington Spa, CV32 4EA, UK.)

woman's womb, who may or may not be its biological mother. So O'Donovan concludes: 'I confess that I do not know how to think of an IVF child except (in some unclear but inescapable sense) as the *creature* of the doctors who assisted at her conception.'[14] That many people today see nothing amiss about producing children this way is surely further evidence of the way consumerist thinking has affected not simply our concepts of right and wrong but our understanding of human nature itself.

It may be argued that modern fertility treatments such as IVF are relatively benign manifestations of a consumerist approach to human reproduction, but it is very difficult to say this about abortion. The former are at least trying to create human life, but there is no doubt that abortion is destroying human lives, most often for merely social reasons. Consumerist considerations are paramount in social abortion. The birth of a child would disrupt one's education or career, would be an embarrassment, limit one's freedom, incur costs and obligations that one cannot face, and so on. For essentially selfish reasons, parents decide their child must die. In 1995 there were 162,447 abortions in England and Wales: of these 156,721 (96%) were done because of 'a risk to the physical or mental health of the mother'. As is well known, this has become the catch-all category that allows abortion for almost any reason, because to deny it might risk the mother's health. No abortions were done in an emergency to save a mother's life or to prevent grave permanent injury to the mother. Just 1,828 (1.1%) were done because of substantial risk of serious disability in the child, i.e. to prevent the birth of handicapped children.[15]

These figures show how far consumerist thinking already governs our attitudes to life and death. If the hallmark of consumerism is individual choice governed by self-interest, abortion shows such choice being exercised in radical fashion. Since the passing of the Abortion Act in 1967, which has virtually allowed abortion on demand, more than four million abortions have been carried out in Britain. To put these totals in perspective: More children have died in British abortion clinics than British soldiers died in the battles of the First World War; soon we shall be able to record the fact that

---

[14] O'Donovan, *Begotten*, 85.

[15] *Life News*, 9.

more have died in our clinics than in Nazi extermination camps in the Second World War.

The wholesale termination of so many innocent lives, mostly for the convenience of their parents, is an affront to anyone with compassion. It is also a total rejection of the biblical and Christian tradition, which sees human life as sacred because humanity is made in the image of God (Gen. 9:6). It is a reversion to the pagan practices of the classical world which tolerated abortion and infanticide.

On the face of it, the 1.1% of abortions done to prevent the birth of handicapped children seem benevolent compared with the heartlessness of social abortion. But closer examination shows that even here consumerist values are taking precedence over traditional biblical ones. Consumerism values good looks, pleasure and comfort above everything else. Handicapped people do not enjoy these to the same extent as the able-bodied. Indeed their quality of life may be such that it is argued that they would be better off dead. And very probably it will cost their families and society a lot to look after them properly, while they themselves will be able to make very little economic return to society. Thus it is kinder to kill them, and it will save money into the bargain. Thus economic logic and consumerist values conspire against the interests of the handicapped.

Now while no one should underestimate the burden of caring for a handicapped person, young or old (four months looking after a handicapped baby drained me and my wife), discriminating against people for this reason is totally against biblical teaching. Both testaments insist that God is especially concerned for the weak, the sick and the disadvantaged and that his people should be too. 'Inasmuch as you did it unto one of the least of these my brethren, you did it unto me' (Mt. 25:40). And throughout Christian history, inspired by the example of Jesus the great physician, the care of the sick and the handicapped has been regarded as a fundamental duty of his followers. And those who suffer are in a special way identified with Christ, who took our infirmities and bore our diseases. The centrality of suffering within human existence and the demand for a compassionate response to it is alien to the whole consumerist outlook, which looks for a pain-free comfortable lifestyle unencumbered by the long-term commitments handicap and illness may bring. Hence the desirability of eugenic abortion to this outlook.

The same consumerist attitude is apparent in the modern campaign to legalise euthanasia, incidentally another practice that was accepted in the ancient world before the coming of Christianity.[16] Consumerism focuses entirely on this world and its pleasures, so that death itself is the ultimate disproof of all that consumers hold dear. It may be for this reason that in our era death is the great taboo topic that people rarely talk about. When it happens to someone near them, they try to pretend it has not happened. Modern funeral practices and mourning customs all seem designed to ensure that the death is forgotten as soon as possible.[17]

Two fundamental tenets of consumerism are encapsulated in the voluntary euthanasia campaign: the avoidance of pain and individual autonomy. (Few today would publicly advocate involuntary euthanasia, though the Dutch experience of allowing the former where it has been requested by the patient suggests it leads quite easily to involuntary euthanasia, where it is performed on the doctor's or relatives' initiative.[18])

Pleasure seeking and self-gratification, the avoidance of risk and discomfort, are all central to the life of the modern consumer. Death may be unavoidable, but we should try at least to avoid a painful

---

[16] That is, if we regard euthanasia as a kind of assisted suicide. It is noteworthy how many 'modern' attitudes addressed in this paper were actually commonplace in the classical world before the arrival of the biblical tradition, e.g. no weekly rest day, easy divorce and remarriage, the right to abortion, suicide and cremation. Tolerance of homosexual practice was also widespread. It would be going too far to say such attitudes and practices were universally approved; rather that they were widely tolerated.

[17] Contrast traditional Jewish mourning practice which insists on a year's mourning for close relatives and that children should light a candle and recite the Kaddish prayer every year on the anniversary of a parent's death. This is seen as obedience to the command to honour your father and mother. Cremation, another pre-Christian custom reintroduced in the nineteenth century, is also suggestive of a consumerist outlook to worn-out products and shows scant respect for a belief that human beings are created in the image of God and destined for resurrection. Jews and Moslems, who also believe in the resurrection of the body, adamantly oppose cremation.

[18] Keown, *Euthanasia*.

death and a pitiful old age. So runs a modern line of thought. Consumerism, which idolises youth, beauty and health, has little respect for the elderly. So when we reach that stage of life, let us cut it short and opt out.

This disparagement of old age is of course quite contrary to the biblical perspective, which admires the elderly for their wisdom, sanctity and perseverance.[19] As we have already observed, the book of Job and the New Testament both hold that suffering may bring one nearer to God. But whereas there were moments when Job expressed a wish to die, that never legitimated him taking measures to bring death nearer. 'Shall we accept good from God, and not trouble?' (Job 2:10) was his response to his wife's suggestion that he commit suicide. On the cross Jesus was offered wine with myrrh as a painkiller, but he refused to drink it (Mk. 15:23). However, it has never been supposed that ordinary people should follow his example at this point, rather Proverbs 31:6 is thought to mandate pain relief to the dying. Indeed, even if some pain-relieving drugs do incidentally hasten death, they may still be administered as long as the primary intention is not to kill the person.[20]

Thus rejecting euthanasia does not mean that some people are consigned to a painful death. But this does not satisfy the hard-line consumerist. They argue, like the hard-line feminist on abortion, that it is their body, so they can decide to do what they like with it. As Clapp observed, the central commitment of consumerism is to 'self-creation and autonomous self-definition'.[21] In the case of euthanasia this autonomy is taken to its *reductio ad absurdum*. The advocates of euthanasia argue that if someone cannot create themself any more, they may at least organise their de-creation. When death is inevitable, they should at least arrange its timing. If it is not a crime to commit suicide, why is it wrong to ask a friendly doctor to help someone do it painlessly and efficiently?

But this argument is incompatible with Christian theology and ethics. Death is not the end, and after death we must face our creator to answer for our deeds done on earth. Furthermore, as we have

---

[19] E.g. Lk. 2:25–38; 1 Tim. 5:1–2.
[20] Jochemsen, *Euthanasia.*
[21] Clapp, *Passion*, 20.

already observed, taking innocent human life is expressly forbidden, as humanity is made in God's image. This means it is as wrong to take one's own life as to take someone else's life. And while suicide may be a purely autonomous act, assisted suicide such as voluntary euthanasia is certainly not. It involves turning the doctor, who is dedicated to bringing life and health, into an agent of death. It constitutes a rejection of the love of friends, family and society, who should be prepared to care for the elderly altruistically. It is ultimately a denial of the love of God for every one of his creatures, however young or old, ugly or beautiful they may be. It is the final expression of despair, an acknowledgement that the goals of consumerism are in the words of Ecclesiastes 2:11 'vanity of vanities', that is, illusory, transient and a 'striving after wind'.

Concluding Observations

We have focused on four areas where Christian ethics and consumerist ethics are at loggerheads: Sunday observance, marriage, abortion and euthanasia. By way of conclusion I want to look at more general aspects of the consumerist package that make it incompatible with the Christian way of life, namely its oppression of the weak and its destruction of virtue.

Consumerism offers freedom, freedom to everyone to be themselves, to do what they like. Personal autonomy, freedom of choice, is the fruit that everyone is invited to pick in the late twentieth-century Garden of Eden called western democracy. But as the secular writers Slater and Miles on the one hand and Christian writers such as Lyons, Clapp and Pope John Paul II on the other have observed, this apparent freedom is really a licence for the powerful to oppress the powerless.

Slater contrasts the values of traditional and consumerist societies. In traditional societies everyone had their place and stayed there. They had certain rights and obligations, and their status determined their consumption patterns. But 'a modern world based on pure individual self-interest ironically leaves the individual in a chronically weak condition. Without a binding collective culture, without solidarity, the individual – isolated, adrift on tides of momentary desires – is open to manipulation and the most subtle forms of unfreedom.'[22] Modern consumers are manipulated by advertisers and small traders are driven to the wall by big business.[23]

Paradoxically consumerism, which promises people freedom and satisfaction, actually needs to make people discontented to promote business. Slater points out that advertising makes people perpetually dissatisfied with their lot.

> Modern need is insatiable because it is no longer fixed either by nature or by the traditional social order. Whereas culture might subordinate need to higher values, consumer culture dreams up ever more needs and enslaves people to a vicious circle of unceasing need feeding off perpetual dissatisfaction. Deregulated society, then, far from providing a moral framework for meaningful individual and collective life, now exercises a deep form of corruption and compulsion over its disoriented members.[24]

Consumerism while apparently offering individual choice, 'actually delivers heteronomy – man's needs are determined by the fashions, opinions and scrutiny of society.'[25]

> Thus Consumer Culture, which to liberalism seemed to be exemplary of individual autonomy, comes to stand for all sorts of slavery: to desire and insatiable needs, to social scrutiny and competition, to political as well as cultural despotism and tyranny. Liberation from social restraint really means the loss of natural feeling and of stable social values and therefore the weakening, disorientation and subjugation of the individual. Society comes to dominate the individual, not least through the material world of objects and interests, which are now essential not merely for meeting needs but for being or finding a self.[26]

If Slater is most concerned about the predatory and manipulative nature of big business, the Pope in his 1995 encyclical *The Gospel of*

---

[22] Slater, *Culture*, 73.
[23] Miles, *Consumerism*, 56–58.
[24] Slater, *Culture*, 77.
[25] Ibid., 78.
[26] Ibid., 83.

Life is most concerned about similar attitudes pervading relationships between individuals.

> When freedom, out of a desire to emancipate itself from all forms of tradition and authority shuts out the most obvious evidence of an objective truth, . . . then the person ends up by no longer taking as the sole and indisputable point of reference for his own choices the truth about good and evil, but only his subjective and changeable opinion or, indeed, his selfish interest and whim.
>
> This view of freedom *leads to a serious distortion of life in society*. If the promotion of the self is understood in terms of absolute autonomy, people inevitably reach the point of rejecting one another. Everyone else is considered an enemy from whom one has to defend oneself. Thus society becomes a mass of individuals placed side by side, but without any mutual bonds. Each one wishes to assert himself independently of the other and in fact intends to make his own interests prevail.[27]

This leads to people compromising to allow everyone some scope to assert themselves.

> In this way, any reference to common values and to a truth absolutely binding on everyone is lost, and social life ventures onto the shifting sands of complete relativism. At that point, *everything is negotiable, everything is open to bargaining*: even the first of the fundamental rights, the right to life.
>
> This is what is happening also at the level of politics and government: the original and inalienable right to life is questioned or denied on the basis of parliamentary vote or the will of one part of the people – even if it is the majority . . . In this way democracy, contradicting its own principles, effectively moves towards a form of totalitarianism. The State is no longer the 'common home' where all can live together on the basis of principles of fundamental equality, but is transformed into a *tyrant* State, which arrogates to itself the right to dispose of the life of the weakest and most defenceless members, from the unborn child to the elderly, in the name of a public interest which is really nothing but the interest of one part.[28]

---

[27] John Paul II, *Gospel*, 35.
[28] Ibid., 35f.

Thus both Slater and the Pope point out that the untrammelled freedom vaunted by consumerism, if it is not limited by convention or divine law, is really a licence for the strong to exploit the weak in society.

Another point both secular and Christian writers agree on is that consumerism destroys traditional virtues. Slater points out that what matters today is not your character but the impression you make on others. 'Instead of being sanctioned by guilt, the other-directed character is driven by "a diffuse *anxiety*" about measuring up to the transitory expectations of others.'[29] The modern consumer is a slave of swiftly changing fashion. 'Paradoxically . . . perpetually hanging on everyone else's good opinion, [he/she] is at the same time self-obsessed.'[30]

The self-obsessed individual wants to be loved rather than esteemed, and this leads to narcissism. 'The narcissist is utterly self-absorbed, obsessed with the relation of every person and event to his own needs . . . driven by a desire for endless gratification, experience, and impulse, but with no possibility of any commitment.'[31]

Clapp, from a Christian perspective, laments the self-centredness of modern culture. He quotes de Tocqueville's analysis:

> I see an innumerable multitude of men, alike and equal, constantly circling around in pursuit of the petty and banal pleasures with which they glut their souls. Each one of them, withdrawn into himself, is almost unaware of the fate of the rest. Mankind, for him, consists in his children and his personal friends. As for the rest of his fellow citizens, they are near enough, but he does not notice them. He touches them but feels nothing. He exists in and for himself.[32]

Clapp agrees with C. S. Lewis that the loss of moral absolutes means that though we want people of principle and virtue, it is impossible to create them in our present climate. 'We clamour for those very qualities we are rendering impossible. . . . We make men without

---

[29] Slater, *Culture*, 90.

[30] Ibid., 91.

[31] Ibid., 93.

[32] A. de Tocqueville, *Democracy in America* (Garden City, N.Y.: Doubleday/Anchor, 1969), 691–2.

chests (i.e. people who no longer believe in goodness and moral order) and expect of them virtue and enterprise. . . . We castrate and bid the geldings be fruitful.'[33]

Clapp ends by contrasting the consumerist pursuit of pleasure and self-indulgence with the Christian way of sacrifice, love for God and for others, and the recognition that this world is not our home.

> From a Christian point of view, then, the path of genuine self-transcendence, of authentic heroism, . . . lies in giving one's self away for the sake of one's neighbor. It is the way of the cross.[34]

Bibliography

Andreasen, N. E. A., *The Old Testament Sabbath* (Missoula: Scholars Press, 1972)

Beckwith, R. T. and W. Stott, *This Is the Day: The Biblical Doctrine of the Christian Sabbath* (London: Marshall, Morgan & Scott, 1978).

Clapp, R., *The Consuming Passion: Christianity and the Consumer Culture* (Downers Grove: IVP, 1998)

Jochemsen, H., *Euthanasia: A Christian Evaluation* (Oxford: Latimer House, 1995).

John Paul II, *The Gospel of Life* (London: Fount, 1995)

Keown, J., *Euthanasia Examined: Ethical, Clinical and Legal Perspectives* (Cambridge: Cambridge University Press, 1995)

Lewis, C. S., *The Abolition of Man* (Glasgow: Collins, 1943)

Lyon, D. A., 'Consumerism' in D. J. Atkinson and D. H. Field (eds.), *New Dictionary of Christian Ethics and Pastoral Theology* (Leicester: IVP, 1995), 256–7

Miles, S., *Consumerism as a Way of Life* (London: Sage, 1998)

O'Donovan, O. M. T., *Begotten or Made?* (Oxford: Clarendon, 1984)

---

[33] C. S. Lewis, *The Abolition of Man*, (1943, reprint, Glasgow: Collins, 1978), p. 20.

[34] Clapp, *Passion*, 39.

Slater, D., *Consumer Culture and Modernity* (Cambridge: Polity, 1997)

Tocqueville, A. de, *Democracy in America*, trans. G. Lawrence (Garden City: Doubleday, 1969)

Vaux, R. de, *Ancient Israel* (London: Darton, Longman & Todd, 1961)

8

Shopping for a Church:
Consumerism and the Churches

Nigel Scotland

Every year twelve billion catalogues are mailed in the United States and the average American child sees twenty thousand advertisements on television.[1] Much of this has been well charted by Tony Walter in his *Need: the New Religion*.

Consumerism is affecting all aspects of society including sex, pornography, holidays, cars, clothes, household gadgets, entertainment, health and leisure, computers and education. In many universities and colleges of higher education students are now 'customers' who are served by the lecturers and support staff. Course leaders now think primarily in terms of what the students ('consumers') want rather than what they need to know.[2] It is therefore no surprise that the western world has become totally consumption oriented with an appetite that devours not merely the products of capitalism but just about everything else, including church.

Following the Second World War, Britain became a consumer-oriented society. Since 1950 magazines have proliferated at twice the rate of the population's growth. However, it was not until the 1980s that Thatcherite values began to hit the churches in a big way. It was then that 'Good Church' guides were first published and some denominations began to circulate free glossy publications and to boost their wares by staging conferences and Bible weeks. More recent marketing drives have also taken to the Internet and independent television networks. The result of all of this is that

---

[1] See Starkey, *Born*, ch. 1.
[2] Kenneson and Street, *Church*, 39.

many church leaders are convinced that in order to survive they must engage in aggressive marketing. The other side of the coin is that potential congregation members ('consumers') go 'church shopping'. Choosing a church is now like exploring the stores and boutiques of the new malls and arcades in our town and city centres. Increasing numbers of those who go out 'churching' on Sundays have several loyalty cards, which they use according to the needs of their spiritual shopping list for that particular week.

It was the disgraced American televangelist Jim Bakker who used to say the secret of a successful church was to find a need and fill it. He certainly went about the task with considerable aplomb, setting up his multimillion dollar 'Heritage USA' theme park, which was intended as a Christianised version of Los Angeles' Disneyland. Among its attractions were 'heavenly fudge shops , 'Bakkeries', Christian hotels, charismatic waitresses and toyshops that sold born-again dolls and teddy bears which recited Scripture. One of Bakker's aides was able to boast that twice as many visitors were patronising Heritage USA each year as were going to the Holy Land! A distinguishing feature of televangelism was its use of telethons, or banks of telephones that were set up not only to counsel and pray about people's immediate needs following the programme, but also to send out books and anointed prayer cloths and to solicit money, this latter aspect 'enabling us to continue to meet the needs of others like yourself'.[3]

In the wake of televangelism's early successes came a clutch of new megachurches whose agendas and mission statements were based on extensive market research in their immediate neighbourhoods. The most prominent of these was Willow Creek on the outskirts of Chicago. This vast complex provides an environment devoid of traditional religious symbolism that enables participants to look in at the Christian faith from the outside without having to engage in ritual or other activities that bespeak commitment. People come in large numbers because they feel comfortable in an unthreatening atmosphere.

In this same period many more traditional churches also began to take more seriously the style and quality of their presentation. One

---

[3] Hoover, *Mass*, 82–87.

such church, with which I am familiar because I have family in the area, is Central Wesleyan in Holland, Michigan. Here there is a vast brick-built auditorium that seats some 4,000 people. The seating slopes gently down to an expansive stage and rostrum area. Set into the wall behind this area is a huge video screen. Not only do the words of the songs come up here, but the background shows soothing motion pictures of mountain scenery, shimmering lakes and glistening sunshine. When the preacher comes to take his turn, not only is the performance that of a polished actor, but his points are writ large on the video screen, still with appropriate background. Outside the church is a lake with a fountain and a substantial school block. There is a large staff with specialists in areas such as counselling, religious education, and marriage and the family. There are small groups which meet during the week that are focused on almost every conceivable need, including those of single parents, recent divorcees and senior citizens. Central Wesleyan Church, Holland, is not untypical of the way in which churches are developing in much of America. Indeed there's another church not very different a few blocks down the road.

In Britain things tend to move a few steps behind the America scene and at a slightly slower pace. Nevertheless, a similar concern to address people's needs and to respond to the market in a more overt fashion is growing in many UK churches. We catch glimpses of it in improved decor, the re-ordering of church interiors, the use of guitars and keyboards or orchestral music, the disbanding of traditional church choirs, the giving up of clerical robes, and even in such things as liturgical dance troupes, counselling teams, and tape libraries of the preacher's recent sermons. In all of these developments there is a symbiotic relationship between the consumers of religion and the marketers of religion. The clergy and church leaders need to bring people into their churches, but at the same time those individuals are shopping around for what most fulfils their expectations and meets their needs.

The Challenge of Consumerism

Confronted with the consumerism of the western world, churches tend to make one of two responses. Either they opt out of the competitive rat race altogether and operate at some fixed point in the past, or they compete fully in the open market for customers. The first of these two reactions regards consumerism as crass materialism, that is, as a part of the world that is passing away and therefore something Christians should not sully their hands with. On this understanding, consumerism is something that Jesus, who 'had nowhere to lay his head' and 'did not lift up his voice or cry out in the streets', avoided. His followers should do the same. They are also of the opinion that because Jesus is who he is, he can speak for himself and does not need his followers to use hard-sell techniques on his behalf.

Christians and churches who adopt this view frequently become reactionary and try to live in a time warp. They attempt to keep things as they supposedly were in the beginning or at some seminal period of church history, such as the first century, Cranmer's England or Calvin's Geneva. Their congregations stick stolidly to the *Tridentine Mass* or *The Book of Common Prayer* and the beauty of Coverdale's melodic psalmody.

Kenneson and Street in *Selling Out the Church* argue that by marketing a personal religion the church is in fact dehumanising it. The whole essence of marketing as they see it is 'an impersonal exercise in brokering self-interested exchanges'.[4] They also emphasise that some of the demands that God makes on our lives are not easily marketable. David Wells, in his provocative study *God in the Wasteland*, makes the point that one can market the church but not Christ, the gospel, Christian character, or the meaning of life.[5] Wells cites an apposite quotation from Karl Barth to underline his contention:

> The Word of God is not for sale; and therefore it has no need of salesmen. The Word of God is not seeking patrons; therefore it refuses price cutting and bargaining; therefore it has no need of middlemen. The Word of God does not compete with other commodities which are being offered to men on the bargain counter of life. It does not care to be sold at any price. It only desires to be its own genuine self, without being compelled to suffer alterations and modifications. . . . It

---

[4] Kenneson and Street, *Church*, 61.
[5] Wells, *God*, 82.

will, however, not stoop to overcome resistance with bargain counter methods. Promoters' successes are sham victories; their crowded churches and the breathlessness of their audiences have nothing in common with the Word of God.[6]

Those who follow Kenneson, Street, Wells and Barth eschew the whole marketing business believing, in the words of E. M. Bounds, that 'while the church is looking for better methods, God is looking for better men.'

Over against this position there are increasing numbers of churches and church leaders who strongly believe that it is right to compete in the free market. George Barna, for example, wrote that 'Jesus Christ was a marketing specialist.' 'Like it or not', he wrote, 'the church is not only in a market but is itself a business.' It has a 'product' to sell – a relationship with Jesus and others, its 'core product' is the message of salvation, and each local church is a franchise.[7] Barna argues that the church must define its services in terms of contemporary needs just as any secular business must.[8] Advocates of this position urge that churches launch an all-out effort to exploit the market with high-pressure sales techniques. Everything has to be constantly updated, refined and improved on. Such marketers justify their approach by referring to the apostle Paul's declaration that to the Jews he became a Jew, to those without the law as one not having the law and to the weak as himself weak so that by all possible means he might save some (1 Cor. 9:19–23).

From this introduction it is clear that there are two sides to consumerism, in so far as it impacts the churches. On the one hand, there are those who believe that marketing Christianity is a contradiction that undermines the core values of the faith. On the other hand, there are those who are convinced that unless churches adopt aggressive advertising and selling campaigns they will lose what little ground they have left. The remainder of this essay considers the implications of these two positions in greater depth.

---

[6] Ibid., 60.
[7] Barna, *Marketing*, 13.
[8] Barna, *Churches*, 107.

The Downside of Consumerism for the Churches

The Cloning of Success

One immediate danger in trying to sell the church is what might be termed the 'cloning of success'. Something works well for one church down the road or in the same town, and immediately other fellowships and denominations change their vision or methods and adopt the latest route to pulling in the customers. Churches that once enjoyed close relationships with others in the locality and were even members of the same denomination begin to view their neighbours as rivals whose competition must be overcome. Many of them seem to survive on what sociologists have termed 'marginal differentiality'. That is, their objectives and ethos are very similar, but they develop a small margin of difference that is just sufficient to distinguish them from their immediate competitors.

Perhaps the greatest downside in ecclesiastical consumerism is the use of soft-sell techniques to market the Christian message. Certain key aspects of the creedal faith, it has to be said, do not market readily; notably the themes of judgement, punishment, suffering for one's faith, the cost of commitment and the demands of taking a public stand on Christian values in a culture that does not acknowledge them. Thus there is always the temptation to tone down or pass over these issues in church adverts, brochures or Web pages on the Internet. At the same time strong emphasis is placed on the more appealing aspects of the worship band, the small groups, the camaraderie of the safe-haven youth groups that will keep teenagers from drugs and sexual misadventure. In a forthright passage Wells urges on the church the need for an authentic and rigorous stand against these kinds of compromise.

> It must give up self-cultivation for self-surrender, entertainment for worship, intuition for truth, slick marketing for authentic witness, success for faithfulness, power for humility, a God bought on cheap terms for the God who calls us to a costly obedience. It must, in short, be willing to do God's business on God's terms. As it happens, that idea is actually quite old, as old as the New Testament itself, but in today's world it is novel all over again.[9]

---

[9] Wells, *God*, 223.

Kenneson and Street strongly endorse Wells' views on the matter. For them the whole church marketing issue is an indicator of how 'worldly' the church has become. As far as they are concerned, if the church is to be an authentic sign of God's emerging kingdom, then it must leave behind accepted secular techniques for promoting its message. The enterprise of church marketing, as Kenneson and Street perceive it, is not a neutral tool. It is a 'value-laden enterprise' or tool that will re-fashion the church in its own image.[10] In short it will change the nature of the product itself.

Talking up the Market and Addictive Christianity

In order to hold onto customers they already have, many churches talk up the market. I recently heard a charismatic Christian express his disillusionment at the way his church had for the past twenty years constantly 'preached the anointing', while holding out the prospect of a great revival just around the corner. When I later questioned him about this, he explained that he felt that the church had used the 'promise of revival' to maintain its grip on the congregation. They did not dare to leave in case the blessing did come and they might miss it.

Philip Richter held that the Toronto Blessing reflected a sense that the novelty of the initial charismatic manifestations had waned. He regarded the phenomena emanating from the Airport church as a last attempt to reinvigorate and rekindle the smouldering embers of the charismatic movement. He backed his claim with evidence that prominent English charismatic church leaders such as Sandy Millar of Holy Trinity, Brompton, and Mark Stibbe, then of St. Mark's, Sheffield, professed to be at a low spiritual ebb in the period immediately beforehand. Richter went on to point out that experienced-based religion is 'a highly marketable product'. The people behind the Toronto Blessing, he maintained, knew their market and 'capitalised on the consumers' demands for a thrills and spills, white-knuckle-ride religion'. He pointed out that 30,000 British pilgrims spent approximately £25 million on trips to Toronto in the summer of 1995.[11]

---

[10] Kenneson and Street, *Church*, 34.
[11] Porter and Richter, *Toronto*, 1–37.

Martyn Percy saw the Toronto form of charismatic experience as 'quick, easy and consumer oriented, a sort of McDonaldization of mysticism'. In fact, while he was at Toronto the blessing was described as 'a spiritual car wash'. Percy saw the whole thing as a bargain freebie in which participants gave up their rationality in return for a warm (sometimes romantic or sexual) feeling. It cost nothing in terms of study, work or prayer, and pilgrims received a reassuring, comforting emotional experience.[12]

Rowland Howard suggests that the whole charismatic movement is based on power and success. He maintains that the Toronto Blessing was 'a desperate cry, a last gasp at self validation'[13] and puts down the charismatic movement's marketing and promotion techniques as an unethical use of modernity's tools to exploit the "market".'[14] The continual use of hype to promote the new experience, the next rising preacher, or conference or event is little more, he maintained, than 'a mirror image of "worldly" consumerism'.[15]

Another means of holding existing congregational members and drawing in other floating customers is the organisation of conferences. Not only do these occasions draw people together in closer comradeship, they're an opportunity for the organisers to promote their wares to those who come from outside their ambit. Perhaps of more serious concern are the large sums of money that the organisers of large conferences are able to pull in and an addiction to conferences on the part of a small but growing number of participants. Some are getting hooked on Bible exposition or worship or the next piece of powerful ministry to a point where other more needful activities are being set aside.

Ensuring that Only the Fittest Survive

One problem of a free-market enterprise among the churches is that inevitably there will be winners and losers. In the end it will be the most aggressive and powerful who will survive and prosper, while the weakest and smallest will go to the wall. All this raises serious

---

[12] Cited by Howard, *Charismania*, 115.
[13] Ibid., 134.
[14] Ibid., 137.
[15] Ibid., 137.

questions since the gospel focuses on one who came to empower the weak and to serve and strengthen the outcasts and the marginalised. Megachurches and fellowships with large congregations have sufficient income to develop sophisticated media advertising and thus to attract a following from a wide geographical area. At one level this can be interpreted as beneficial, since it provides an opportunity for community and religious experience that may not be available to people in their own locality. On the other hand, it draws people away from smaller churches and may in some cases result in the closure of these churches. In this context Max Weber's 'hinterland theory' seems poignantly relevant. Weber observed that the greater the distance people travel to a place of worship, the greater is the decline in the influence of that religious institution or organisation. Thus it could be argued that overtly aggressive marketing by churches, if it is siphoning members from other congregations rather than reaching outsiders, is probably dysfunctional in the long term.

Changing Both Clergy and People

This constant pressure to market the church more and more effectively inevitably carries a price tag with consequences for both church leaders and their members. Traditionally and in the New Testament, the local church has been seen as a tightly-knit fellowship with the members bound together in commitment, love and practical caring and under the pastoral supervision of their leader or leaders. In recent years, however, all of this has begun changing; church leaders are no longer pastors but marketers and managers, and many congregational members are ceasing to be committed serving members. Instead they become church shoppers.

Because of the pull of market forces there is now constant pressure on churches to employ pastors or incumbents who are good managers and know how to run a successful business. As Barna put it, 'Ultimately, many people do judge the pastor not on his ability to preach, teach or counsel, but on his capacity to make the church run smoothly and efficiently.'[16] Put starkly, Barna argues that in essence

---

[16] G. Barna, *Marketing the Church* (Colorado Springs: Nav Press, 1988), p. 14.

the pastor is judged as a businessman. Kenneson and Street argue that it is not only market forces that have exerted constant pressure on the minister or clergy person to be a manager or marketer. Equally influential has been his or her declining role as a local theologian. Gone are the days when pastors were respected for their theological insights and learning. Theology has been largely hijacked by the academics who see it as their preserve, with the result that many congregational members now regard it as irrelevant to everyday needs. Indeed many look for church leaders who have only a minimal grounding in academic theology but who instead have expertise as psychologists, trained counsellors, therapists or organisers. To put it in the words of Bryan Wilson, for many their primary function is to be 'a general affective agent'.[17]

It is not merely the leaders of churches who are changing their roles; the same is true of potential members. Because the churches are marketing their product in such an aggressive fashion, people are minded to keep looking round in case they missed out and there are better bargains and services to be had at St. Develictus-in-the-Marsh on the other side of town. Consumerism has created a generation of church shoppers who move from one fellowship to another in the same way that grocery shoppers change from Tesco's to Safeways to Sainsbury's to Waitrose to Gateway and back. In the same way churchgoers move as the ads and the grapevine prompt them. All of this, it is argued, produces a jaundiced church, which is far removed from the deeply committed fellowships that formed the backbone of the early church.

Privatising Religion

To sum up, the downside of consumerism in contemporary Christianity is that it has resulted in rampant individualism. Indeed Andrew Walker has charted how 'ascetic individualism' (doing good) has given way to 'hedonistic individualism' (feeling good).[18] In America this development has manifested itself in the prosperity teaching of individuals such as Kenneth Hagin and Gloria and

[17] B. R. Wilson, 'God in Retirement', *The Twentieth Century* (Autumn, 1961, No. 24), 170.
[18] Walker, 'Consumerism'.

Kenneth Copeland. Their health-and-wealth gospel urges us 'to name it and claim it' or, in the words of Oral Roberts, 'You sow it, God will grow it.' Indeed, wealth is seen as a sign of God's favour and blessing so it's little wonder that many evangelists have no conscience about drawing large salaries and swanning round in large cars with personal assistants at their sides and mobile phones in their pockets.

Starkey has pointed out that even though many Christians do not endorse prosperity theology, they have nevertheless taken on board much of its consumer worldview.[19] Thus the starting point of many has become my needs, my self-interest and my satisfaction. Much of contemporary evangelism tells people Jesus will make them happy and fulfilled. People therefore look for a church that meets their needs and they go to worship for what they can get out of it. Indeed the comment 'I didn't get much out of that service' is often passed without even a thought that there might have to be a sacrifice of praise and thanksgiving or a concerted effort to worship God with all of one's heart, mind, soul and strength. Thus for many churchgoers Christianity has become primarily a lifestyle, an ethos, a culture or a club, rather than a faith or relationship with a Lord who demands total commitment on the part of his followers and who wants them to live in community relationships with others.

The Benefits of Consumerism

Although, as we have seen, consumerism has engendered a host of adverse side effects, its impact on society and on church life is by no means all bad. Indeed, in secular terms, consumerism has brought in its wake better health and housing, affordable food, clothing and transport. There can be no doubt that the physical quality of life is vastly improved, far above what it was a hundred years ago. The same is true of Christian churches; consumerism has provoked and stimulated improvements in many areas. Even Wells is prepared to state at one point that 'we do indeed have to take the notion of a religious market seriously because it may well explain why some movements succeed and others fail.'[20]

---

[19] M. Storkey, *Born to Shop*, 222–7.
[20] Wells, *God*, 67.

Clarifying vision

A major benefit of the present market orientation is that it has caused churches to consider carefully what it is they're trying to sell and how they can best go about it. For example, a church that is going to open its own Web site may find itself compelled to reflect on what is distinctive in its vision and how it should set out a mission statement. One group of church marketers recommend defining a church's mission in terms of customer groups, customer needs and alternative technologies. They state:

> A helpful approach to defining mission is to establish the congrega-
> tion's scope along three dimensions. The first is its customer groups
> – namely, *who* is to be served and satisfied. The second is its customer
> needs – namely, what is to be satisfied. The third is alternative
> technologies – namely, how persons' needs are to be satisfied.[21]

There is much to be said for seeking to meet people's needs. In particular, to do so is a servant-oriented ministry and Jesus called his disciples to follow his example of service to others. In Mark 10:45 Jesus stated that his mission was not to be served but rather to serve and to give his life a ransom for many. After having demonstrated what service meant in a very visual way by washing his disciples' feet he called on them to do the same for one another and, by implication, others outside their immediate circle (Jn. 14:13–17). George Barna urges that offering to meet people's needs is not a marketing gimmick but a 'method of ensuring effective ministry'.[22] The key issue here, it seems to me, however, must be to distinguish carefully between a person's 'perceived' need and their 'genuine' need. Some 'needs' may prove to be selfish, materialistic and indeed unbiblical. It cannot be right to work towards satisfying what are in essence wrong desires.

Barna urges every church to develop a 'vision' and to focus on it repeatedly until it is firmly rooted in the mind of the congregation. By vision he understands a clear mental picture of the future which

---

[21] Shawchuck, Kotler, Wrenn and Rath, *Marketing*, 89.
[22] Barna, *Churches*, 107.

is not humanly contrived but which has been sought from God. Each church's vision will be distinctive and customised to its immediate setting and goals. Barna argues that such mission statements are what change churches and enable them to grow and develop.

It seems to me that marketing a church by means of a specific vision and mission statement that sets out the finer details in bullet points or succinct paragraphs can only be beneficial, always assuming that the biblical creedal faith is not compromised in any way. Clearly anthropocentric strategies or therapeutic models that soft-pedal the issues of sin and Christian morality are to be eschewed. But given these provisos, a clearly stated mission is not only an asset but has dominical precedent. Jesus clearly came 'to be about his father's business', he knew that he had a baptism to be baptised with, he set his face steadfastly to go to Jerusalem, he only did what he saw the Father doing and he cried out 'Father, not my will but your will be done.'

Calling to Service

Jesus clearly established a new model for leadership and disciple-ship; both were to be servant ministries. A great deal of what marketing the church has been and is about is seeking more effective ways of serving the needs of congregations, communities and localities. It has been frequently said, and with justification, that many Christians and churches are scratching people where they do not itch. The kind of market research that is being done using structured questionnaires has, at the very least, generated an aware-ness of the gaps that exist between churches and those they would like to serve. This divide, in many instances, has to do not so much with matters of faith and order but rather of style, ethos and cul-tural relevance. Some churches have removed traditional symbols such as crucifixes, icons and statues that outsiders might find intim-idating. Bare boards have been carpeted and pews have been replaced by comfortable movable seating. In some instances the whole sanctuary has been reordered with pulpits and choir stalls removed. Clergy have shed their robes and vestments and worshippers have been encouraged to dress-down. New church buildings have on occasion been constructed to resemble shopping malls or airport lounges. Such moves seem eminently sensible since their objective is to provide a more familiar environment in which people can engage with the Christian message.

Of course church marketers carry their desire to serve beyond the level of mere aesthetics. They conduct surveys that often reveal high degrees of brokenness in particular localities. The problems include debt, unemployment, inadequate housing, marital breakdown, dysfunctional families, loneliness and fear. In addition, there may be ethnic and racial tensions together with a rundown physical environment that fosters a culture of drugs, violence and petty crime. For congregational leaders to be aware of the level and extent of such issues can only widen the possibility of a more effective ministry.

The idea of developing a servant ministry based on such surveys has not been without its critics. Kenneson and Street argue that it often serves the ends of marketing rather than God's kingdom.[23] Ferdinand Tönnies suggests that such service often proves to be self-interested, based on the principle 'I give so that you give'. However, provided that these and similarly misplaced motivations are avoided, it would seem both valid and right for churches to seek and to serve what market research reveals as manifestly genuine needs. This was clearly a guiding principle in Jesus' life and ministry. He fed hungry crowds, he healed the sick and he changed water into wine to save the face of the caterers at a wedding in Cana.

Challenging Apathy

There comes a stage in every religious institution that sociologists term 'routinisation'; that is, when the original 'charisma' and enthusiasm of the leadership begins to run down. At that time there is a temptation to put the whole package – doctrine, worship, vision and ministry – into a fixed pattern or ecclesiastical straitjacket. The advantage of this is that no further effort is required. However, the problem is that within a generation the whole movement will be in decay and facing a lingering death. Vance Havner, formerly of Wheaton College, Illinois, charted this process of decline as follows:

---

[23] Kenneson, and Street, *Church*, 68.

'It begins with a man; soon there emerges a movement; then a machine takes over; and finally there remains only a monument.'

One of the benefits resulting from ecclesiastical marketing is the reminder that because the surrounding needs and culture are constantly changing, the churches need to continually reassess their environment and strategies. A Church of England diocesan bishop has expressed his gratitude for the many so-called 'new churches' that are springing up in different parts of the UK. 'They challenge Anglicans,' he said, 'to rethink the ways in which they are doing church.' Clearly the church is in the debt of those of the Gospel and Culture movement and those who survey and seek to quantify genuine local need. They are the agents who help to provoke the people of God to authentic action and service.

Niche Marketing

One aspect of consumerism is what is frequently termed 'niche marketing'; that is, a customised, individual approach that is designed to reach particular groups of people who have distinctive tastes and values. We see it, for example, in the selling of newspapers and magazines. The tabloids aim to reach one segment of the population and the broadsheets another. The same is true of package holidays: Thompsons aim primarily to attract younger families and singles in their twenties and thirties, while Simply Crete or Manos Holidays are more focused on Greek culture, and so on. The success of confined marketing enterprises has positive implications for the churches. Some church planters, for example, have established new congregations with the specific objective of reaching a particular people group, or ethnic minority or designated age bracket. This kind of precise targeting has proven to be an effective means of evangelism and has seen the emergence of unique enterprises such as the 'Soul Survivor' network of youth churches (headquarters in Watford) and Revelation Youth Church in Chichester.

Niche marketing widens the appeal of a particular product to a greater number of people by repackaging it in distinctive styles for varying contexts. In the same way, churches have been enabled to reach a greater number of constituents by using variations of this model.

Redeeming the Culture

Church marketers spend a good deal of their energies in studying the culture in order that they may more effectively present the Christian message in a manner that resonates with it. Clearly it is incumbent on those who study the culture then to conduct a rigorous assessment of that culture from an informed biblical perspective. This process should enable churches to distinguish between people's 'artificial' needs and their 'basic' or real needs. The former should not be responded to. In addition, the analysis will give the church the opportunity to redeem the culture. In this way it will be able, in an authentic manner, to be 'salt' and 'light' and to Christianize the social order

Postscript

Clearly Christians and church leaders must be constantly engaged in the task of analysing their surrounding culture and the perceived needs of the people who live within it. Such an exercise is demanding, and some may be tempted to give up the ongoing struggle and to stick with 'the old-fashioned, unchanging gospel'. Critics of church marketing continue to urge that this is a science of compromise. It must be acknowledged that, on occasion, it may be so. Nevertheless it is my firm conviction that it is possible to market the gospel using consumerist models without necessarily changing the product. It is also possible to embrace some aspects of postmodern culture without allowing the world to squeeze us into its mould.

In conclusion, we must recognise that success and successful methods are no valid criterion by which to judge anything, marketing included. Nevertheless, the church is surely in a more effective position when it blends good marketing practice with wholehearted commitment to Christ and the biblical Christian faith.

Bibliography

Barna, G., *Marketing the Church: What They Never Taught You about Church Growth* (Colorado Springs: Navpress, 1988)

—, *User Friendly Churches* (Ventura: Regal Books, 1991)

Hoover, S. M., *Mass Media Religion* (London: Sage, 1998)

Howard, R., *Charismania* (London: Mowbray, 1997)

Kenneson, P. D. and J. L. Street, *Selling Out the Church: The Dangers of Church Marketing* (Nashville: Abingdon, 1997)

Porter, S. E. and P. J. Richter, *The Toronto Blessing – Or Is It?* (London: Darton, Longman & Todd, 1995)

Shawchuck, N., P. Kotler, B. Wrenn and G. Rath, *Marketing for Congregations: Choosing to Serve People More Effectively* (Nashville: Abingdon, 1992)

Starkey, M., *Born to Shop* (Eastbourne: Monarch, 1989)

Walker, A., 'Consumerism, Personhood and the Future of Christian Mission', a paper read at the Seduction or Evangelism conference (9th Feb 1998) at Cheltenham & Gloucester College of Higher Education

Walter, T., *Need: The New Religion* (Leicester: IVP, 1985)

Wells, D., *God in the Wasteland: The Reality of Truth in a World of Fading Dreams* (Leicester: IVP, 1994)

9

The Toronto Experience in a Consumer Society

Graham A. Cray

The Toronto Blessing is so called because it originated in an outpouring of the Spirit that began at the Airport Vineyard (now Airport Christian Fellowship) Toronto in January 1994. My own perspective is not one of detached analysis because my wife and I had this experience in the summer of 1995. However, I have always been committed to serving my own tradition through constructive criticism and aim to do the same in this chapter, using the tools of both theology and social analysis.

Responses to the Phenomenon

Since 1994 there have been varied responses to the Blessing ranging from 'mass hysteria' or 'purely psychological', to 'a time of refreshing from God' and even 'the foretaste of revival', to 'demonic deception' or 'resolving the charismatic movement's mid-life crisis'. Various critiques and defences of the Blessing have been made.

Some responses have been of little help. For example, dismissing the Blessing as 'all psychological' ignores the fact that the action of the Spirit upon our humanity cannot but include characteristics that can be analysed by the tools of psychology. Those tools are not designed to identify the action of the Spirit through our psychological makeup.

Some responses have been naive, amounting to no more than trivial proof-texting for or against. Others have imposed inappropriate criteria through their choice of analytical tools (e.g. Philip

Richter's use of rational choice theory[1]) or have been reductionist (e.g. Martin Percy's use of the theory of social exchange[2]). Richard Middlemiss's criteria in *Interpreting Charismatic Experience*[3] contain some good theological sense, but offer little more than negative guidelines to interpretative practice. Their aim is to reduce what he sees as exaggerated charismatic claims to a more rational level, but the guidelines offer little for the positive discernment of the Spirit. I believe the whole subject raises significant questions about discernment and the interpretation of religious experience which will become increasingly necessary as the postmodern era develops.

Toronto and Postmodernity

If charismatic Christianity contains anti-modern, modern and postmodern features, as the editors of a recent collection claim,[4] and if the Toronto Blessing is regarded as having more of a postmodern perspective, then it is clear that some responses to it demonstrate an inadequate grasp of the major shift in cultural context being experienced in the west at the moment. Harvey Cox sees the whole global Pentecostal movement as the forerunner of a postmodern age:

> The Pentecostal movement provides us with an invaluable set of clues, not just about the wider religious upsurge but about an even more comprehensive set of changes. These changes are not just religious ones, they add up to a basic cultural shift for which the overtly spiritual dimension is not just the tip of the iceberg but the stream in which the iceberg is floating. A major refiguration of our most fundamental attitudes and patterns which will ultimately alter not just the way some people pray but the ways we think, feel, work and govern.[5]

---

[1] Richter, *Toronto*, 104. In my view, applying rational choice theory to this type of Christian activity introduces presuppositions into the analysis that seriously distort its findings.

[2] Percy, *Toronto*.

[3] Middlemiss, *Experience*.

[4] Hunt, Hamilton and Walter, 'Tongues', 4.

[5] Cox, 'God', 48f.

If Cox is right, the tools of modernity will be of only limited use for an assessment of the Blessing. But whatever we make of Cox's claims, we need to place any assessment of the Toronto Blessing in the context of western society's current period of transition from modernity to postmodernity.[6] Postmodernity is characterised by the elevation of consumer choice to the integrating value of society; by an electronically globalised society that takes everything everywhere – radically increasing the apparent range of consumer choice – and by a profound distrust in rationalism and suspicion of large-scale shared frameworks of understanding. It is within such a world that the gospel has to be proclaimed, that the Spirit will act, and that the church will have to exercise discernment.

It will not do simply to decry consumerism and all the other changes. Fish might as well decry the quality of the water they have to swim in. However justified their complaints, they still cannot get out of the water! Whatever our views of postmodern culture, and I am one who believes it offers as many opportunities as hazards, it is the era in which we live, and the place where we are called to contextualise our faith while trying to avoid syncretism. Any attempt at contextualisation worth the effort will inevitably run close to syncretism at some time! Accusations of conformity to the world need particularly careful attention at a time of social transition. Charismatic Christianity has been accused of inconsistency because 'it appears to resist secularising forces while simultaneously endorsing some aspects of present day culture.'[7] But this is precisely what is required of any informed Christian mission. The important question are what is resisted and what is endorsed, and on what basis?

Religious Consumerism?

Among the more interesting analyses and critiques of the Toronto Blessing have been those from a sociological perspective which see the Blessing as a form of religious consumerism. This I will address

---

[6] See Walker, *Story*, chs. 6–7; Lyon, *Postmodernity*.
[7] Hunt, Hamilton and Walter, 'Tongues', 3.

first; then in the second part of the chapter I will follow through my conviction that theological and doctrinal categories and presuppositions must be primary in the exercise of discernment about any claimed initiative of the Spirit, and also provide the only appropriate context for analysing sociological and psychological insights. I will also suggest the importance of engaging with the history of Christian spirituality.

To begin with, however, I will examine the relationship of the Blessing to our western consumer culture. Andrew Walker, a friendly critic of charismatic renewal, has argued that

> the Charismatic movement . . . has in fact been for the spirit of the age rather than against it. It has perhaps . . . capitulated to the consumer and experiential hedonism of late modernity and become commodified and corrupted. It has arrived, at the dawn of the new millennium, as no longer reluctantly or thoroughly modern, but ultra or hyper-modern.[8]

So to what extent has charismatic Christianity, as manifested in the Blessing, become a religious form of 'experiential hedonism'? Contemporary consumers have been described as 'sensation gatherers', and it is true that at the heart of charismatic convictions is the belief that the Spirit of God is an experienced reality. To some critics this conviction has been confused with the consumer tendency to seek immediate satisfaction. One writes: 'the movement has increasingly appealed to members of a society who have grown up with the three-minute culture of the television and have come to expect instant satisfaction. . . . It satisfies an impatient demand to consume experience now.'[9] This and the other aspects of consumerism considered below are inevitable temptations for those who live in a consumer society. But most charismatics are also committed to living scripturally in the postmodern world, and our profound conviction is that the Spirit is a person to be experienced. In our view, as Gordon Fee has written in his magisterial summary of St. Paul's teaching on the Spirit, 'it must be candidly acknowledged not only that the experience and life of the Spirit were for the most part more

---

[8] Walker, 'Modern', 34.
[9] Hunt, Hamilton and Walter, 'Tongues', 12.

radically in the centre of things for Paul and his churches than for most of us, but that the Spirit was a more genuinely experienced reality as well.'[10] Charismatics are right to emphasise the experiential dimension of Christian faith and, simultaneously, in danger of losing the New Testament tension between what we already experience and what is not yet complete. In the New Testament the one who was 'in the Spirit on the Lord's day' shared with his fellow Christians not only 'the kingdom' but also 'the persecution' and 'the patient endurance'.[11] Nevertheless, a form of Christian discipleship that expects to experience the God it serves is vastly to be preferred to one that restricts itself to rational explanation or liturgical texts alone. (All three are necessary!)

A Craze?

Another dimension of consumerism is the tendency to live for the latest in music, fashion or whatever. Andrew Walker has said of the Blessing that 'sociologically . . . it has been a craze'.[12] In an innocent sense this is true. Whether at Toronto, Sunderland, Holy Trinity – Brompton, or New Wine, it was what we focused our energies on for a period of time. But this says nothing about its authenticity or origin. If God's Spirit was in it, we were right to focus our energies accordingly. There is, however, a more substantial warning to be heeded. A group of sociologists of religion have pointed out how

> postmodern society produces . . . a culture in which what matters is not what is true or what is meaningful, but pzazz, what catches the eye, for only that which catches the eye will sell. If religion is to compete in a postmodern world it too must offer eye-catching wares, which is precisely what neo-Pentecostalism does. God has to top last year's eye-catching interventions in this world with something even more eye-catching this year.[13]

---

[10] Fee, *Presence*, 896.
[11] Rev. 1:8–10.
[12] Walker, 'Modern', 35.
[13] Hunt, Hamilton and Walter, 'Tongues', 12.

Clearly God is not competing in the consumer market, but could this aspect of consumer culture have deceived or even distorted the vision of those of us who sought the Blessing. The answer, I believe, is both yes and no. Yes, the charismatic movement has a history of 'crazes', of current emphases, often in themselves helpful but sometimes giving the impression of keeping the movement going rather than waiting for the Spirit. The desire for 'the latest' has sometimes distorted discernment and resulted in a degree of incredulity. Some of the peripheral phenomena around the Blessing and some of the practices of some leaders should, I believe, have come under more careful scrutiny. Andrew Walker points out that we live in a society that has replaced 'mere Christianity with the merely strange'.[14] But no, this does not discredit the core of what was taking place, or deny the activity of God in it. We simply need to remember that the purpose of gifts from God is spiritual maturity, rather than being 'tossed back and forth by the waves, and blown here and there by every wind of teaching'.[15]

Self-Indulgence?

The temptations that accompany religious experience include self-indulgence, making the pleasure of the experience an end in itself. We live in a culture concerned with the self and its satisfaction, with personal fulfilment and the meeting of individual needs. Because God cares for us as whole people, these issues are not outside his concern, but they can be used to subvert his purposes. Christopher Lasch warned us that 'the contemporary climate is therapeutic not religious. People hunger not for personal salvation . . . but for the feeling, the momentary illusion, of personal well-being.'[16] The theologian David Wells warns of 'the triumph of the therapeutic over the moral even in the church' and rightly points out that

> the New Testament never promises anyone a life of psychological wholeness or offers a guarantee of the consumer's satisfaction with

---

[14] Walker, 'Modern', 18.
[15] Eph. 4:7–14.
[16] Lasch, *Culture*, 7.

Christ. . . . As beings made in God's image we are fundamentally moral beings, not consumers. The satisfaction of our psychological needs pales in significance when compared with the enduring value of doing what is right.[17]

All of this is right, but the accusation that 'the consumer goals of happiness, health and personal fulfilment painlessly accompany the Blessing' is a caricature.[18] It focuses on experiences without reference to the fruit they can bear and ignores the new ministries to the lost and the poor, and the renewed emphasis on intercession that has resulted in many churches. Paul makes it clear that an authentic mark of the Spirit's activity is seen when believers identify more fully with the Spirit's groaning over a broken world.[19]

Philip Richter sounded a more helpful note of warning in pointing out that our society has largely thrown off a former (indirect) Christian influence, what Max Weber called 'the Protestant ethic', and that 'the 1960s counter-culture replaced "goodness morality" with the "fun morality" of a more permissive society.'[20] Charismatic Christianity in the west has to be understood in the context of a society that has grown less inhibited about physical and emotional experiences, but that has also moved away from self-denial in the direction of hedonism. Richter points out that 'the form taken by the Blessing (for instance, spiritual drunkenness) fits with the changing approaches to bodily disinhibition in late capitalist society.'[21] A certain loss of inhibitions is not the worst thing that could happen to many western churches! However, it is vital to maintain the essential connection between experiences of the Spirit and Christlike behaviour. Paul states that those who live by the Spirit 'will not gratify the desires of the sinful nature'.[22] There is no New Testament promise more important for the charismatic movement than this. The ultimate test of any claimed work of the Spirit is its long-term impact on character.

---

[17] Wells, *Wasteland*, 115.
[18] Richter, 'Mysticism', 120.
[19] Rom. 8:18–27.
[20] Richter, 'Mysticism', 119f.
[21] Richter, *Toronto*, 107.
[22] Gal. 5:16–26.

At its most hedonistic, the ideology of consumerism is opposed to every underlying value the Christian faith stands for. A recent book asserts that

> pleasure lies at the heart of consumerism. It finds in consumerism a unique champion which promises to liberate it both from its bondage to sin, duty and morality as well as its ties to faith, spirituality and redemption. Consumerism proclaims pleasure not merely as the right of every individual but also as every individual's obligation to him or her self. . . . The pursuit of pleasure, untarnished by guilt or shame, becomes the new image of the good life.[23]

The use of such religious language by two secular academics is striking. In such a society, charismatics will be tempted to live for religious experiences as a sort of feel-good factor. However, I have no reason to believe that the majority who benefited from the Blessing succumbed to that temptation. What the church needs today is a new confidence in the power of the Spirit to transform the character and behaviour of those who come to know Christ,[24] not a fearful withdrawal from religious experience because of the seductions of consumerism.

Globalisation

We live in a globalised world. One aspect of consumerism is that it appears to offer great choice, but in fact the same brands are available wherever you go. Consumer choice sometimes seems to mean you can get McDonald's everywhere. This standardising and homogenising of western-influenced cultures has been described by one scholar as the McDonaldisation of society.[25] Because the

---

[23] Gabriel and Lang, *Consumer*, 100.

[24] 1 Cor. 6:9–11.

[25] Ritzer, *McDonaldisation*. Ritzer's thesis needs to be treated with considerable care. It is an application of Weber's theory of rationalisation which in its initial form took no notice of social theory about postmodernity. A further volume (*The McDonaldization Thesis*) utilises postmodern theory while rejecting the notion that these are 'epochs that follow one another' (118). In my view, this is itself inadequate and also oversimplifies the complex relationship between postmodernity and globalisation.

Blessing spread largely from Toronto and was experienced all over the world in fundamentally similar ways, Philip Richter has suggested that it 'could be interpreted as a process of "McTorontoisation"'.[26] This is an amusing play on words containing a half-truth. The phenomena experienced in the Blessing all have precedents in former revivals, and in the world of video, television and the World Wide Web. It is not surprising that a certain standardising of expectations should occur. However, there are also reports of outbreaks of similar spiritual manifestations in places that had no knowledge of Toronto. More serious, though, was a tendency among some of those ministering to people to standardise assumptions about the meaning of different manifestations. Just because people have the same physical or emotional experiences does not mean that the Spirit of God is doing identical things in them. The New Testament implies that the initiatives of the Spirit are particular to each person, as well as being for the sake of the whole church.[27]

If the Blessing did turn out to be a self-indulgent seeking after spiritual experiences for their own sake, rather than a response to a new initiative of God in his church, then the outcome for many would be a deep sense of disillusionment. Experience apart from a coherent framework of belief leaves you empty. The novelist Douglas Coupland was speaking for many of his own generation when he asked 'is feeling nothing the inevitable result of believing in nothing?'[28] Part of the significance of the Blessing was the fact that it was located in a clear biblical framework of belief in the promises of God for the outpouring of the Holy Spirit, who does not disappoint.[29]

The Consumer Worldview

Consumerism is not merely a way of life, but is increasingly recognised as a framework through which people find their identity and

---

[26] Richter, *Toronto*, 114.
[27] 1 Cor. 12:7–11.
[28] Coupland, *Life*, 177f.
[29] Rom. 5:5.

sense of belonging in society. 'Where once westerners might have found their identity, their social togetherness and the ongoing life of their society in the area of production, today these are increasingly found through consumption. It's not that companies are producing less, or that people no longer work. Rather, the meaning of these activities has altered.'[30] Consequently consumerism forms a worldview which demands attention.

Firstly,[31] *consumerism focuses our attention on the present rather than the past or future.* 'To live for the moment is the prevailing passion – to live for yourself, not for your predecessors or posterity.'[32] Those Christians who, through the Blessing, focus on the latest thing they believe God to be doing need the reminder that 'to many in the postmodern era the "now" and the "new" have no sense of continuity nor church history, no patience with dogma nor ecclesiastical authority.'[33] Mature Christianity recognises the significance of tradition and authority and values a sense of history; at least so that it can avoid repeating history's mistakes. The Blessing made no sense apart from its place in the ongoing work of God in Christ. We have no way to assess the totally novel.

New Testament teaching about the Spirit also maintains a tension between the already experienced and the not yet experienced.[34] The Spirit is both the power for the present and the one who sustains us for what is to come.[35] He is the source of hope,[36] not the one who 'takes the waiting out of wanting'. It is unfair to characterise all those who experienced the Blessing as failing to take this tension seriously, but it is a danger for any experience-based spirituality.

---

[30] Lyon, 'Memory', 284. It is at this point that I disagree with Slater, *Consumer* (see Craig Bartholomew in the Introduction to this book) who, I believe, confuses the origins of consumption with its changed social meaning as a component of postmodernity.

[31] The following points are complementary to those outlined by Craig Bartholomew in the Introduction.

[32] Lasch, *Culture*, 5.

[33] Hunt, Hamilton and Walter, 'Tongues', 12.

[34] For a detailed summary of this 'eschatological' tension in St. Paul's theology of the Spirit, see Fee, *Presence*, especially ch. 12.

[35] Heb. 6:4–6.

[36] Rom. 8:18–25.

Secondly, '*consumer society is individualistic by definition.*'[37] The consumer's right to choose is the highest value and the focus is on the individual rather than the community. In the New Testament, manifestations of the Spirit are given to build up the church.[38] My own observation of those who sought the Blessing was that they wanted to be part of what the Spirit was doing in the church, rather than just seeking their own spiritual satisfaction.

Thirdly, *consumerism emphasises feeling over thinking.* So Andrew Walker warns of 'charismatic Christians' . . . growing tendency to allow experience to become the touchstone of orthodoxy' and that 'this touchstone is not a return to New Testament Christianity, as is believed, but a thoroughly late modern concern with the self and its satisfaction.'[39] The warning is fair, but the issue is not so simple because the Bible describes and promises an experienced truth. Similarly David Middlemiss warns that 'within the Charismatic movement reason and theology may be used in defense of an interpretation of experience, but essentially the experience has priority, and is justification in itself.'[40] This does happen and is a challenge to those who exercise a teaching ministry within the charismatic movement. However, it is again a vast oversimplification, rooted perhaps in a desire to return to an Enlightenment view of rational certainty that is no longer credible.

What is clear is that the process of discernment as to what is and is not of the Holy Spirit demands clear biblical and theological frameworks, and that some reactions to the Blessing showed that these need to be substantially strengthened. As Andrew Walker has said 'for many touched by Toronto it has been impossible to interpret it with the theological tools to hand.'[41]

A Challenge to Discernment

In fact much that was experienced at Toronto was familiar. For those experienced in charismatic renewal, there is in one sense

---

[37] Sulkenen, *Society*, 6.
[38] 1 Cor. 14:12.
[39] Walker, 'Modern', 36.
[40] Middlemiss, *Experience*.
[41] Walker, 'Modern', 35.

nothing particularly new about what happened. An encounter with God that has some emotional and physical characteristics lies at the heart of classical Pentecostal spirituality (the largest communion of Christians in the world after the Church of Rome!). It has had a much more overt place in the charismatic movement during the last decade, largely as a result of John Wimber's ministry. However, the Toronto phenomenon was the fastest development yet experienced in UK charismatic renewal. It spread very quickly indeed and involved clergy and congregations who did not previously consider themselves to be 'charismatic'. It has faced Christian leaders with new challenges about discernment.

Certain of the phenomena were new, unusual, or disproportionate in comparison with previous experience. 'Laughter in the Spirit' was not new, nor was 'resting in the Spirit', but these manifestations were much more dominant than before. Other, stranger phenomena such as roaring like lions or growling like bears were new, somewhat puzzling, and definitely open to question, but these constituted only a small proportion of the manifestations. The critics of the movement have tended to emphasise these factors out of all proportion to their actual occurrence and significance.

There is a sense in which this experience proved 'contagious', in the sense of being passed on and reproduced in the ministries of those who received prayer themselves. To what extent were we experiencing a sovereign initiative of God that was not entirely dependent on a sort of succession? The laying on of hands as a form of commissioning and imparting blessing has good theological grounding. What has concerned some critics is the involvement of two teachers with 'Faith Movement'[42] connections and unorthodox theologies in the events leading up to January 1993 in Toronto (the teachers are Benny Hinn and Rodney Howard-Brown). However, this presupposes a pipeline theory of influence – that if you had hands laid on you by someone who had hands laid on them by someone whose theology was heterodox, then you yourself came under some sort of deception.[43]

---

[42] For heterodox influences on the thinking of the Faith Movement, see McConnell, *Gospel*.

[43] I find this as theologically unacceptable in charismatic form as I do the equivalent pipeline view of apostolic succession for ordination.

A significant factor can be identified in the servant quality that has characterised the ministries of many of the churches and networks that have been involved in this ministry. The statement of purpose of the Airport Vineyard is 'to live in the love of God and to give it away'. This they have done with extraordinary stamina and commitment since 1994. Both Holy Trinity, Brompton, and St. Andrews, Chorleywood, have made great efforts 'beyond the call of duty' to share what they believe they have received.

As a consequence of Toronto, charismatics have rediscovered pilgrimage. But Zygmunt Bauman has contrasted pilgrimage as a secular metaphor of modernity with tourism as a metaphor for postmodernity.[44] A critical question would be: Were the thousands who went to Toronto fleeting tourists seeking the latest spiritual excitement at the latest spiritual hot spot, or were they those with a vision of God's future, seeking renewal by the Spirit who is the foretaste of that future? In all probability, both aspects were present, even within the same person, but charismatic Christians are pre-modern in their commitment to a revealed faith that links the actions of God in the past to present experience and thus to hope for the future. Despite the blandishments of a consumer society, they have a narrative identity that predisposes them towards pilgrimage in its traditional sense.[45]

The ambiguity of spiritual experience and its relationship to a consumer culture point to the need for discernment, which is also necessary because genuine encounter with God is by definition risky.

> For Pentecostal Christians . . . *dangerous presence* is the ideal starting point for an exploration of our spirituality. . . . Encountering God is of course inherently risky not only because God is so much greater than we are, but because it cannot leave us unchanged. The folk spirituality of the West is quite clear that God is acceptable provided he does not unsettle us.[46]

---

[44] Bauman, *Life*, 92–99.

[45] For the concept of narrative identity, see the writings of Paul Ricoeur, in particular *Oneself*, 140–168.

[46] Adrian Chatfield, unpublished paper for Anglican Renewal Ministries.

Discernment is also necessary because apparent experiences of the Spirit are not self-authenticating.[47] However, attempts at discernment merely by justifying or condemning phenomena or by assessing the extraordinary miss the point. The key question is: 'What is the primary function and purpose of *any* encounter with the Spirit?' In addition, most responses to the Blessing have been limited to assessments of the authenticity of the events (Is this God or not?) without raising questions of the adequacy of the interpretation of them (To the extent that this is God, how are we to understand and respond to what he is doing?). It is this second question which I believe to be the more fruitful.

A good example of the trivialisation of discernment was the furore over those who were said to 'roar like lions.' In the primary literature on revival there are frequent references to 'roaring'. When John Wimber asked members of his church about their experience, they made no mention of 'like a lion'. This was an interpretation added later, and then texts about lions were quoted as a quite spurious justification. Others rejected the Blessing because people fell backwards and, in their view, in the Bible people who encounter God fall forwards!

Both critics and participants were frighteningly thin on theological frameworks for understanding experiences of the Spirit. My viewpoint is that Toronto was a blessing because it at least contained an initiative of God's Spirit to his church. I also believe that many who experienced God in this way had an inadequate Christian worldview for a full grasp of the significance of their experience. We can grieve, resist or quench the Spirit through theological illiteracy just as much as through conformity to consumer culture.

Frameworks for Discernment

The following would seem to be the most significant doctrinal factors to provide a theological worldview that would act as a basis for both discernment and discipleship.[48]

---

[47] See Dunn, *Jesus*, ch. 10.

[48] A theological worldview involves both intellectual frameworks and their resulting praxis (see N. T. Wright, *Testament*, 122–126). Understood in this way, a worldview both precedes and includes the 'kingdom perspective' Craig Bartholomew correctly calls for in his Introduction.

The Trinity

All experiences of the Spirit have a trinitarian setting; to the Father, through the Son, by the Spirit (Eph. 2:18).[49] Experiences of the Spirit are never for their own sake. They are experiences of the Son actualised by the Spirit to deepen our awareness of the relationship we have with the Father. The prayer 'Come Holy Spirit' is valid to the extent that it is understood in this trinitarian context. It is not possible to separate the action of the Spirit from the purposes of the Father or the mission of the Son. The Spirit is self-effacing, directing attention to the Son and through the Son to the Father (Jn. 14:26; 15:26; 16:13–15). He catches us up in the Son's relationship with the Father because we are 'in Christ'.[50] Charismatics desire experience of the Spirit and the Spirit is to be experienced; but the experience then points us away from the Spirit. 'Our desire for God did not originate with us. We did not initiate the possibility of this relationship. The Trinity made it possible and kindled the desire within us.'[51] Experience of the Spirit sought entirely for its own sake is a form of conformity to a contemporary culture of 'sensation gatherers' that majors on the 'feel-good factor' and only seriously engages with the present.

Transcendence and Immanence

Some critics accuse the charismatic movement of reducing encounter with God entirely to the category of God's immanence, encouraging a cosiness with God at the cost of any sense of transcendence and awe. 'The God of the Charismatics is above all an immanent God who acts in the world.'[52] This may be true of the unconscious self-understanding of some, and therefore of some

---

[49] This is both an exegetical and a doctrinal claim. There is an implicit trinitarianism in the New Testament that leads to the doctrinal formulations of the first four centuries. These creedal formulations then throw light on the implications of the biblical text. For the trinitarian dimension of Paul's theology of the Spirit, see Fee, *Presence*, ch. 13. For the trinitarian implications of the New Testament as a whole, see Turner, *Spirit*, ch. 11; Pinnock, *Flame*, ch. 1.

[50] See Torrance, *Worship*, chs. 1–2; Cocksworth, *Holy*, ch. 7.

[51] Pinnock, *Flame*, 46.

[52] Richter, *Toronto*, 100.

understandings of the Toronto Blessing. However, it is foreign to the heart of the tradition and, if anything, the dramatic nature of some recent experience has substantially heightened the sense of awe. God's Spirit as sovereign transcendent presence is a more adequate theological category and better fits the actual experience. 'Talk of the Spirit is not a way of speaking of God's immanence, but of his transcendence. (The Spirit may be active *within* the world, but he does not become a *part* of the world).'[53] 'Acts represents the Spirit as the transcendence of God, over, to, and through the church. The Spirit is the God who cannot be gagged. For Luke the Spirit is not the immanence of God in the church: the Spirit is virtually always rather the self-*manifesting* presence of God.'[54]

The Eschatological Spirit

Christian experience of the Spirit has an already/not-yet tension within it. It can never be triumphalist; it is present experience to sustain hope for the not-yet and to enable identification with pain and suffering. The Spirit is 'the *certain evidence* that the future had dawned, and the *absolute guarantee* of its final consummation.'[55] The Spirit is the first–fruits of the harvest which will be reaped at the end of the age (Rom. 8:23). He is the down-payment, the first part of what will be received in full when Christ returns (2 Cor. 1:22; 5:5; Eph. 1:14). He is the seal which guarantees 'the day of redemption' (2 Cor. 1:21–22; Eph. 1:13; 4:30). He is the present dynamic power of the future age (Heb. 6:4,5; Acts 1:8; 1 Cor. 4:4). Because he is first–fruits not final harvest, first instalment, not the fulfilled kingdom, his ministry through Christians, like his ministry through Jesus, is not unambiguous, automatically convincing or with overwhelming force, but is a pointer or sign of the kingdom. 'The action of the Spirit is to anticipate, in the present and by means of the finite and contingent, the things of the age to come.'[56] This anticipation of the future is holistic, it integrates assurance, sanctification and empowering for service in the context of the certain hope of the coming kingdom. It is God-centred, for the sake of the world.

---

[53] Gunton (referring to John Zizioulas' view), *Spirit*, 123.
[54] Turner, *Power*, 439.
[55] Fee, *Presence*, 806.
[56] Gunton, *Promise*, 68.

All of this has always been true of the best of Pentecostal and charismatic spirituality.

> Here and now, there and then are telescoped and traversed by the Spirit so there is a personal impact of the already-not yet tension in the affective response and observed behaviour. Pentecostals who are moved deeply and powerfully by the Spirit will laugh and cry, dance and wait in stillness. In the Spirit they 'already' participate in the marriage supper but also live in the 'not yet' of a lost world. . . . But every fulfilment, every 'already', has an overplus of not yet or promise. . . . This intensification of joy means also an intensification of sorrow or longing. The sorrow is the affective recognition of the 'not yet'.[57]

Note that in this quotation both the 'already' and the 'not yet' are experiences; there is joy and longing. This is not the same as a distinction between 'subjective' experience and 'objective' rationality.

Where the already/not-yet tension is lost, the result is either triumphalism or a world-avoiding escapism. It is of particular significance to some of us who have 'laughed in the Spirit' that our experience has resulted in a deepened capacity to empathise with the pain of others and makes us quicker to tears than to laughter. This outpouring is occurring at a time of significant cultural transition and unease in the west. From a sociological perspective, such experiences have often occurred at times of social displacement. The crucial question is always whether the outcome is renewed strength to engage with the work of God in the world or to evade it.[58]

The Eschatological and Epistemological Work of the Spirit

The western tradition of theology has majored on the Spirit's epistemological function, that is, on the fact that the Spirit's primary purpose is to communicate reliable information about God. This has given birth to two children. The first is a rationalistic liberalism

---

[57] Land, *Spirituality*, 98f.
[58] See Lewis, *Religion*.

that rightly fears the 'irrational', but which often confuses it with the intuitive or non-linear and treats emotion with suspicion. The accusation that the Blessing is 'nothing but hysteria' shows some evidence of this perspective, with its concern that 'it will lead to the undermining of an intellectually respectable expression of faith.'[59] The second is a rationalistic evangelicalism that in effect limits the Spirit's action to illuminating the Bible. This confuses the Bible's final authority in matters of doctrine with teaching and preaching, which is one significant means by which the Spirit encounters us with the realities of which Scripture speaks. On this basis the Toronto Blessing has been denounced in part because of a few alleged incidents when 'manifestations of the Spirit' prevented the preacher from delivering his message.

By contrast both the Orthodox and Pentecostal traditions stress the Spirit's eschatological work as outlined above; the breaking of the future kingdom into present experience in a wholistic but partial and anticipatory fashion. To a certain extent these two valid traditions of pneumatology have been arguing past one another, but the eschatological provides a fuller understanding of the Spirit's work and in fact includes the epistemological, because 'now we know only in part; then we will know fully, even as we have been fully known'.[60]

Pentecost and Calvary
The already/not-yet tension in experience of the Spirit can only be sustained by relating the gift of the Spirit to the finished work of the cross. The Spirit empowered Jesus to offer himself on the cross (Heb. 9:14). The Spirit could not be given to those who believe until Jesus had been glorified (the cross, resurrection and ascension seen as a whole in John 7:39). Once given, the Spirit places Jesus' intimate name for the Father upon the believer's lips (Rom. 8:15f., Gal. 4:6). But 'Abba' is a Gethsemane word (Mk. 14:36). The Spirit anoints experientially for the purpose of costly obedience before the kingdom comes in its fullness. The Spirit is the power by whom Jesus was raised from the dead at work in believers (Rom. 8:11).

---

[59] Robert Jeffrey – Church Times.
[60] 1 Cor. 13:12.

The power of the Spirit is the power of the resurrection that we may live the lifestyle of the cross. (Phil. 3:10f.). As Tom Smail emphasises, the Spirit flows from the cross and all of life in the Spirit is cross-shaped.[61] 'The way to Pentecost is Calvary. The only power the Spirit has to give is the mysterious power of the cross that keeps on manifesting itself in weakness.'[62]

David Wells defines the negative biblical meaning of 'the world' as 'fallen humanity en masse, the collective expression of every society's refusal to bow before God, to receive his truth, to obey his commandments, or to believe in his Christ . . . the public context in which fallen life is lived out.'[63] In postmodern society 'the world' in this sense is consumer-shaped. The doctrine of the cross is the strongest safeguard against the temptations of consumerism. Translated into a life of discipleship, the cross is the means by which 'the world has been crucified to me, and I to the world' (Gal. 6:14).

The Spirit and the Humanity of Jesus

To what extent is Christ's charismatic experience a model for our own expectations? The New Testament and some subsequent christologies (Owen, Irving, Smail, Gunton[64]) suggest that our Lord's ministry was through the empowering by the Spirit of his humanity, not the direct action of his deity through his humanity. If this is the case, his experience provides a paradigm for us. It also follows that the Spirit frees us to be truly human. Authentic experience of the Spirit will then have some parallels with the experience of Jesus and will be authentic to the extent that it frees us to grow into a more Christlike humanity.

Martin Percy makes an important point when he refers to Torrance's warning against 'a chronic tendency to thrust Christ into the majesty of God and neglect his continuing ministry in our humanity.'[65] Similarly, Pete Ward, in his study of evangelical songbooks in *Growing Up Evangelical* points out that *Songs of Fellowship* focuses massively upon Christ's resurrection, heavenly

---

[61] Smail, *Once*, 26, 112.
[62] Smail, *Windows*, 117.
[63] Wells, *Wasteland*, 37–39.
[64] See Schwöbel and Gunton, *Persons*.
[65] Percy, *Words*, 79.

rule and promised return with 'little or no reference to the incarnation . . . the earthly life of Jesus has to be subsumed in the concentration on the risen Lord who reigns from on high.'[66]

Where such an inadequate framework is in place, the consequence is likely to be either a dualistic detachment of spiritual experience from everyday life or a triumphalistic expectation of God's action replacing our frailty and weakness. But Percy is, I believe, quite wrong when he accuses Wimber-influenced charismatics of having a theology of power as 'supernatural brute force, rather than the ambiguous power of Calvary'[67]. However, his general point still needs to be taken.

These theological emphases on the trinity, the eschatological Spirit, the cross and christology all raise issues of power, for each contributes to and controls the content given to 'the power of the Spirit'. There is a substantial responsibility on those who lead times of 'ministry in the Spirit' to teach that authentic spiritual power is always in weakness rather than replacing weakness, and to model ministry that is neither manipulative nor dependent on the power of suggestion. However, I must affirm that the ministries that I have observed were exemplary in this matter. There is also an inevitable 'no win' situation in which necessary leadership that enables those present to respond to God with understanding and to interpret what is happening in a meeting is viewed by some as manipulation or suggestion.

The Particularity of the Spirit's Work
There has been great emphasis on the Spirit as the source of unity but less on the diversity of the Spirit's actions in gifting and encountering each Christian in the particular way that is appropriate for them and necessary for the kingdom. This allows for the apparent 'confusion' of diverse manifestations, including laughter and tears, occurring at the same time. It also warns against the danger of limiting the Spirit's actions to an over-narrow list of current Toronto phenomena. On this understanding, the mark of a manifestation of the Spirit is that it does not overwhelm the freedom and integrity of the person.

---

[66] Ward, *Evangelical*, 136.
[67] *Words*, 79.

Creation and Redemption in a Christological Framework

Creation and redemption, natural and supernatural find their coherence in Christ, and the Spirit is the Spirit of Christ. However, some charismatics and some of their critics betray a tendency towards dualism: a split between natural and supernatural, creation and redemption, the body and emotions set over against the rational mind. Some charismatics do not have an adequate concept of the natural order, seeing everything as the direct action of God or of the Devil,[68] and are threatened by critiques using psychological or sociological categories. Some critics seem to think that an analysis on such grounds rules out the possibility of the action of the Spirit, or at least renders it unnecessary. Some of those involved in the current move of the Spirit share Jonathan Edward's distinction between the actions of the Spirit and human responses to those actions. This allows for a much more nuanced assessment of the phenomena. In particular, Patrick Dixon's view that the Toronto phenomena fit into the category of states of altered consciousness, but that this in itself says nothing about their origins is far more satisfactory.[69]

The Christian grand-story holds together creation and redemption in the unchanging purposes of God. Because of the value of the original creation, the fallenness of the stewards of creation requires a 'new' creation through the cross and by the Spirit. Creation through the Spirit (Gen. 1:2) was merely the start of a committed relationship to the earth. 'God's commitment is a continuing personal activity that supports the created order.'[70] Not only creation but the human cultural enterprise are under Christ's authority (Mt. 28:18) and the realm of the Holy Spirit. 'We share a world where Christ continues to rule through the Holy Spirit so that culture as well as creation is upheld by his presence.'[71] The Spirit sustains culture as well as bringing it to judgement (Jn. 16:7–11). Finally, the whole of the human person is the realm and concern of the Spirit's work of sanctification (1 Thess. 5:23).

---

[68] See N. Wright, *Face*, ch. 6.
[69] Dixon, *Signs*, ch. 5.
[70] Dyrness, *Earth*, 36.
[71] Ibid., 83.

What is needed is a more integrated, embodied spirituality. The physical and emotional encounters undergone in the Blessing are a reminder to white, rationalistic westerners of their profound need of personal integration. There is, I believe, a potentially therapeutic element to the Toronto experience. One black minister commented 'the only thing that surprises me is the colour of the skin!' For Harvey Cox, the original Pentecostal outpouring at Azusa Street marked a breakthrough in such integration:

'In retrospect we can also describe the (Azusa Street) revival as the principle point in western history at which the pulsating energy of African American spirituality . . . leaped across the racial barrier and became fused with similar motifs in the spirituality of poor white people. It marked the breaking of the barrier that western civilisation had so carefully erected between the cognitive and emotional sides of life, between rationality and symbol, between the conscious and unconscious strata of the mind.'[72]

In future a white, rationalistic, analysis of spiritual phenomena can no longer be trusted to stand alone. However, if white, largely middle-class Christians are experiencing a new level of personal integration and being put in fuller touch with their bodies and emotions, we need to ask what levels of pastoral support are also being made available after ministry has been received.

Historical Spirituality

The test for any development in Christian spirituality must include, but not be bounded by, the history of Christian spirituality. Sarah Coakley made a helpful contribution to the report *We Believe in the Holy Spirit* by linking the gift of tongues to the contemplative tradition.[73] Similarly, Michael Mitton began to interpret Toronto from a number of perspectives from the history of spirituality.[74]

One crucial test of authenticity is the quality of holiness that results. Holiness does not arise from emotional experiences alone, but it can arise (in part) from profound encounters with God that

---

[72] Cox, *Fire*, 99f.
[73] Church of England Doctrine Commission, ch. 2.
[74] Mitton, *Heart*.

involve the whole person. Very appropriately many of the clergy involved in the Blessing have studied Jonathan Edwards' criteria for the marks of an authentic work of the Spirit.[75] Edwards work refers to the 'affections' that result from a genuine encounter with God. By 'affections' he does not mean emotions but the deepest desires of the whole person oriented towards Christ and his kingdom.

One difficulty about discernment and religious experience is that the fruit of an integrated godly character takes time to grow and will always be imperfect in this life. The final authentication of any movement of God must await the verdict of church history and then, more importantly, the final verdict of heaven.

Conclusion

We live in a consumer society. Any contextual form of Christian discipleship must be 'in but not of' consumerism. A prophetic counter-cultural discipleship that reflects the values of Christ's kingdom[76] will not evade the world of consumption, but will refuse to find its identity in it, or to use its values as criteria to assess spiritual experience.

I am personally convinced that the Toronto Blessing has been the vehicle of a significant movement of God's Spirit as we enter the consumer age. As such it represents the action of God through our humanity. It is therefore open to both misunderstanding and abuse, and also to analysis with the tools of the human sciences. I am equally convinced that the most significant question about any such spiritual experience is not 'is it from God or not?', but 'what are we to do to discern correctly and respond appropriately?' If my own analysis is right, this initiative has caught us all out. It has challenged many theological assumptions of the non-charismatic part of the church and revealed its rationalism. The tools of social science have helped to reveal its potential and, in some cases, actual weaknesses. But the tools of the human sciences shaped in modernity are not always appropriate to reveal the contours of authentic Christian

---

[75] Edwards, 'Distinguishing Marks' and *Religious Affections*.
[76] See Craig Bartholomew's 'Introduction', 9ff.

experience in postmodernity; so I believe the interpretation of the Blessing as primarily shaped by the narrative of consumerism is seriously misguided. But this movement of the Spirit has also shown the charismatic movement its need of better biblical and theological presuppositions and frameworks to interpret the actions of the Spirit, and the relationship of God to the world and to human culture. Only when our thinking is fully shaped by the full narrative of what Father, Son and Holy Spirit have done and continue to do in creation and new creation will we properly discern and live in the Spirit.

Bibliography

Bauman, Z., *Life in Fragments* (Oxford: Blackwell, 1995)

Church of England, Doctrine Commission, *We Believe in the Holy Spirit* (London: Church House Press, 1991)

Cocksworth, C., *Holy, Holy, Holy: Worshipping the Trinitarian God* (London: Darton, Longman & Todd, 1997)

Coupland, D., *Life After God* (New York: Pocket Books, 1994)

Cox, H., *Fire From Heaven* (New York: Addison Wesley, 1995)

—, 'Why God Didn't Die', *Nieman Reports* 47:2 (1993)

Dixon, P., *Signs of Revival* (Eastbourne: Kingsway, 1994)

Dunn, J., *Jesus and the Spirit* (London: SCM, 1975)

Dyrness, W., *The Earth Is God's* (New York: Orbis, 1997)

Edwards, J., 'The Distinguishing Marks of a Work of the Spirit of God' in *Jonathan Edwards on Revival* (Edinburgh: Banner of Truth, 1965)

—, *The Religious Affections* (Edinburgh: Banner of Truth, 1986)

Fee, G., *God's Empowering Presence* (Peabody: Hendrickson, 1994)

Gabriel, Y. and T. Lang, *The Unmanageable Consumer* (London: Sage, 1995)

Gunton, C., *The Promise of Trinitarian Theology* (Edinburgh: T. & T. Clark, 1991)

—, *The Spirit in the Trinity* in *The Forgotten Trinity* (London: BCC/CCBI, 1991)

Hunt, S., M. Hamilton and T. Walter, 'Introduction: Tongues, Toronto and the Millennium' in S. Hunt, M. Hamilton and

T. Walter (eds.), *Charismatic Christianity: Sociological Perspectives* (New York/Basingstoke: Macmillan, 1997), 1–16.

Land, S., *Pentecostal Spirituality: A Passion for the Kingdom* (Sheffield: Sheffield Academic Press, 1993)

Lasch, C., *The Culture of Narcissism* (New York: Warner, 1979)

Lewis, I. M., *Ecstatic Religion* (Harmondsworth: Penguin, 1978)

Lyon, D., 'Memory and Millennium' in T. Bradshaw (ed.) *Grace and Truth* (Grand Rapids: Eerdmans, 1998)

—, *Postmodernity* (Buckingham: Open University Press, 1994)

McConnell, D. R., *A Different Gospel* (London: SPCK, 1988)

Middlemiss, D., *Interpreting Charismatic Experience* (London: SCM, 1996)

Mitton, M., *The Heart of Toronto* (Cambridge: Grove Spirituality Series 55, 1995)

Percy, M., *The Toronto Blessing* (Oxford: Latimer Studies 53/54, 1996)

—, *Words Wonders and Power* (London: SPCK, 1996)

Pinnock, C., *Flame of Love* (Downers Grove: IVP, 1996)

Richter, P., 'Charismatic Mysticism' in S. E. Porter (ed.) *The Nature of Religious Language* (Sheffield: Sheffield Academic Press, 1996)

—, *The Toronto Blessing – Or Is It?* (London: Darton, Longman & Todd, 1995)

Ricoeur, P., *Oneself as Another* (Chicago: University of Chicago Press, 1992)

Ritzer, G., *The McDonaldisation of Society* (Thousand Oaks: Pine Forge/Sage, 1993)

—, *The McDonaldization Thesis* (London: Sage, 1998)

Schwöbel, C. and C. Gunton, (eds.), *Persons Human and Divine* (Edinburgh: T. & T. Clark, 1991)

Smail, T., *Once and for All* (London: Darton, Longman & Todd, 1998)

—, *Windows on the Cross* (London: Darton, Longman & Todd, 1995)

Sulkenen, P., J. Holmwood; H. Radner and G. Schulze, *Constructing the New Consumer Society* (Basingstoke: Macmillan, 1997)

Torrance, J., *Worship, Community and the Triune God of Grace* (Carlisle: Paternoster, 1996)

Turner, M., *The Holy Spirit and Spiritual Gifts: Then and Now* (Carlisle: Paternoster Press, 1996)

—, *Power From On High* (Sheffield: Sheffield Academic Press, 1996)

Wells, D., *God in the Wasteland* (Leicester: IVP, 1994)

Walker, A., *Telling the Story* (London: SPCK, 1996)

—, 'Thoroughly Modern: Sociological Reflections on the Charismatic Movement from the End of the Twentieth Century' in S. Hunt, M. Hamilton and T. Walter (eds.), *Charismatic Christianity: Sociological Perspectives* (Basingstoke/New York: Macmillan, 1997), 17–42

Ward, P., *Growing up Evangelical* (London: SPCK, 1996)

Wright, N., *The Fair Face of Evil* (London: Marshall Pickering, 1989)

Wright, N. T., *The New Testament and the People of God* (London: SPCK, 1992)